THE ULTIMATE INTERNET OUTLAW

THE ULTIMATE INTERNET OUTLAW

How Surfers Steal Sex, Software, CDs, Games, and More Top-Secret Stuff on the Information Superhighway

Robert Merkle

PALADIN PRESS ¥ BOULDER, COLORADO

Also by Robert Merkle:

The Ultimate Internet Terrorist:
    How Hackers, Geeks, and Phreaks Can Ruin
    Your Trip on the Information Superhighway . . .
    and What You Can Do to Protect Yourself

The Ultimate Internet Outlaw:
How Surfers Steal Sex, Software, CDs, Games, and
More Top-Secret Stuff on the Information Superhighway
by Robert Merkle

Copyright © 1999 by Robert Merkle

ISBN 1-58160-029-1
Printed in the United States of America

Published by Paladin Press, a division of
Paladin Enterprises, Inc.,
Gunbarrel Tech Center
7077 Winchester Circle
Boulder, Colorado 80301, USA.
+1.303.443.7250

Direct inquiries and/or orders to the above address.

PALADIN, PALADIN PRESS, and the "horse head" design
are trademarks belonging to Paladin Enterprises and
registered in United States Patent and Trademark Office.

Visit our Web site at www.paladin-press.com

CONTENTS

v

WARNING
Do you want to go to prison?
If not then read this warning before you go one step further!

LET'S FACE IT: A HOW-TO BOOK ON computer technology (especially networking) can bore a Federal judge out of his socks. That's why this book is meant to shock you out of deep sleep. Hell, brother, this book could bring you out of an alcohol-induced coma.

But be warned! Ignoring my PROLIFIC warnings throughout the text won't go unnoticed by the Federal government for long. If you do decide to attempt any of the techniques herein please, PLEASE contact a lawyer or your local police department first.

Why? Because pirated software is a no-no. Let's be clear. Copyrights are enforced for a reason: to protect the rights of hard-working artists and software engineers. You're a thief if you do anything described in this book, and a court-of-law experience will open your eyes to this in a hurry. Believe me. I know.

What could happen to you?

You could do prison time. Just ask ex-hacker Fibre Optik, a 19-year-old who thought the world of copyrights was a joke. You could incur fines that would reduce you to a quivering mass of jelly. A penniless quivering mass of jelly.

Then there's the possibility of being banned by a federal court from owning a computer of going near a computer outside of the workplace for the next decade. They use probation officers to enforce this. Trust me.

A felony rap is not good if you, say, want the finer things in life. Like a JOB.

One last caveat. While I have written this book specifically for laypersons (those without a degree in computer science), some of you may feel like you stepped in halfway through the movie. You may have no idea what in the hell is going on.

This book is for users with intermediate knowledge of the Internet. If you don't know what "WWW" means, you may need to read a book designed for people just starting out, or talk to a friend who can show you the ropes.

As a checklist, you should already know how to:

- start a dial-up session to your ISP
- open a new browser window (for multiple browser windows)
- download compressed software off the Internet and to successfully decompress it.

If you're shaky about the above three points, your chances of getting anything useful out of this book are slim. Please read a book on subjects such as beginning to use desktop PCs and learning to surf the WWW before proceeding.

PREFACE

"Stolen waters are sweet, and bread eaten in secret is pleasant."

—Hebrew Bible

"It isn't necessary to imagine the world ending in fire or ice—there are two other possibilities: one is paperwork, and the other is nostalgia."

—Frank Zappa

A WORD FROM OUR SPONSORS

I GUESS YOU WILL NEVER know him—John Minnery. I never knew him either. But I read many of his books and I'll never forget them. Christ, the adventures he took me on! I stumbled across his little-known works well over a decade ago, and I'll never be able to reproduce the sense of mystery he gave me. That was a time when the world was haunted by the specter of the Soviet Union amassing all their military might against us, like some evil alien world that would consume every fiber of our existence. A time when the American president propounded that there existed just two countries: THEM and US. A time when it could have happened—where we would have come down to the last bullet and the last tank . . . and the last ICBM.

It was a strange time. And it seemed a little more than possible that I might find myself shooting at Russians even younger than I was in some Godforsaken shithole in Europe.

John Minnery's books fit right into that time. God did they ever! He seemed to have it on the nose. Hell, that guy could show you anything, it seemed to me then: everything from blowing up an armored car with garbage bags, water, and a can or two full of miner's carbide lamp fuel to building a handgun from a nail and block of wood. He could tell you the exact manner of picking a lock with a toothbrush to modifying a laser-pointer to crash a helicopter. It was a time when everyday Joes like me could have used that knowledge to disrupt that ever-feared Russian invasion of the North American continent. The one *everybody* thought about back in those dusty, dead days of 1984.

But times changed. The Russians, it turned out, were A) just as human as us, and B) broke. Instead of being marauders, they immigrated legally and started the Russian Mafia in all the major metropolitan U.S. cities. In doing so, they joined the ranks of untold hundreds of other productive legal immigrants with a history not unlike the Italian immigrants of past centuries.

My vast collection of John Minnery books went up on a high shelf, my fantasies of taking out Russian infantry troops with homemade nerve-gas grenades evaporated, and I went to college. No invasion. No Russians. No Armageddon. It was ended. I went on to get a degree or two. Now, instead of shooting Russians, I baby-sit overgrown silicon diodes.

I never knew John, and I never will. He died several years ago, so the chance to just drop him a line and say "thanks" has passed me by. I suppose my descendants before me had their Rudyard Kiplings and their Sir Conan Doyles to entertain them, but for me it was always J.M. My collection of his books is still there. I take them down once in a while, reading them cover to cover, trying to remember what it was like that first time he showed me how to rig a car to explode or the proper technique to kill a man with a plastic lunch fork. No, a time for me and him to sit down over a cup of hot tea and talk of the intricacies of a small guerrilla band taking out the Russian military and other schemes of forbidden human endeavors will never come, but his books live on.

And for that I thank him. That's fitting, I suppose, since his books are the only side of the man I ever knew. What more there was to John Minnery, hell, I can't say; but I do know this: he took me through many wild races through landscapes of forgotten things, sitting on old patent shelves—things nobody knows about. Except him and me.

Here's to you, J.M. It's only a pale imitation of your works, but this is my way of finally answering your literary "hello."

So let's do this. Let's hit this sucker out of the ballpark.

INTRODUCTION

I'LL NEVER FORGET the day I bought my first computer. You should've seen me—I was out of my skull with ecstasy. After researching which model had the best guzungas for the dough and wasn't going to fry the second day out of the box, and after talking to a million different friends, I found THE RIGHT COMPUTER.

Saving the cash for my new toy wasn't easy. Hell, you know the story—sure you do. We've all got the same sad story. We've got our sorry butts to put through college, a car to pay off, and all the other horrors of modern life. And with this in mind it isn't a whole heck of a lot of fun to spend $2,000 on something that wouldn't give a rat's behind if you died the next day. But eventually we all take THE PLUNGE. You know the one. That foray into a huge, electric mega-lo-mart bubbling with digital electronic toys—the kind of store where time ceases to exist and your credit card nearly runs off on its own will, filling your cart with Ultra DMA hard drives, video games, and God knows what other manner of electronic nightmares. And that's what I did: I took THE PLUNGE. The big one. Not the one for an Ultra DMA hard drive or the latest CD by some asshole with money enough to purchase Bolivia, oh no . . . the one where you buy your first computer.

They see you coming. Sure they do. Not the store clerks

(those retards), but the companies that build the things in the first place. You've heard their vile names before: Compaq, Packard Bell, Hewlett-Packard, CTX, and all the rest. They know you're coming to buy their latest POS, and they're glad. And I delivered myself into their hands . . . just like you did. I know you did since you're reading this. You're just like me. Another sucker.

"So what did you get?" my friend DJ asked.

"A POS 9000," I shot back, still aching to rip it out of the box and smoke check it with all its prepackaged software. God, it looked great! "With 310 megs!" I added, for effect.

DJ smiled and nodded. He knew the name. "Hmmm . . . nice." He walked over and peered at the box with what I assumed was mutual awe. "What are you gonna run on it?"

My smile faltered a little. "What d'you mean? All of it, DJ. Everything out there. Even 'Nightmare from Silicon Valley.' The 3D version that came out last week."

DJ peered at the box for a few more seconds. "Whoaaaa . . . hold on there, Huxstable. Your POS 9000 didn't come with a 3D video card."

My smile came to a screeching halt. It was like those dual rubber tire tracks you see on the freeways . . . the big ones where you can make out the tread of the tire. 3D video card? Shit. It didn't. I was sure that it had.

"You were sure because that's what the sales retard told you, right?" DJ peered at me over the rims of his silver glasses. His eyes were resigned, but understanding; he'd been down this road many times. He was a veteran of this game.

"Well, I mean, yeah, I think, he may have . . . but it's still great, though, you gotta admit that."

"Sure, you don't need 3D to get some great games. Looks great otherwise."

My heart started up again and I felt the familiar anxiety steal over me. It *was* fine. It had great disk storage, a 14.4 modem, 8 MB RAM, and a 16-bit sound card. Who the fuck needed that 3D card anyway?

"That 33.6 modem is gonna be great for surfing," DJ

chimed in, waking me out of my fantasy land where computers were just as standardized and stable as color TV sets and any one was just as good as another in the long strokes of it.

"Ummm . . . it has a 14.4, DJ."

He looked at me as if some faceless horror were just behind my shoulder. Then the look was gone and a new one came in its place. This new look was the same type you would wear to address a child who had severe mental retardation and were straining to get through to. "A 14.4," he whispered and then covered his mouth quickly, as if he had inadvertently uttered an extreme profanity. "Great."

"But an upgrade's a snap," I said, breaking the uncomfortable silence. "And that 14'll get me on for a month or two."

He nodded. "Sure. I can do the upgrade for you if you want."

So things were back on track. Wonderful, I thought, now we can take this baby out and . . .

DJ was rooting around in my plastic "World of Computers" shopping bags. He came out with a virus-scanning utility program bundled with a ton of other applications. "What's this?"

I smiled. He was pleased that I had thought ahead enough to get a virus scanner up and running before I did anything else. That's what I thought.

DJ looked up at me with his eyebrows arched. "You can't run this on your computer." He said the words slowly, as if talking to someone from another country that had a minimal grasp of English.

"What?" I snatched the box out of his hands—literally ripped it right out from where he was holding it—and read the specifications side panel that told the buyer the minimum system requirements to run the program. It required 16 megs. I nearly screamed. I had eight. Eight was good, though, my mind chattered, still trying to salvage something of that two grand. Eight was what they said in all the magazines devoted to computer nerds from hell like yours truly. Eight eight eight.

(Sixteen. Minimum. Don't buy a computer without at least 16 megs or you're screwing yourself and smiling. Thirty-two.

Sixty-four. One-hundred twenty-eight, as of this writing, is what you *should* be buying. Or you're screwing yourself and smiling. Like me.)

I didn't scream. Instead I sat down and tried to tell myself how everything was OK; everything was going to work out. DJ would upgrade the modem. He was a friend and that's what friends were for—to exploit as needed. And the video card. And the RAM. And the hard-drive when that 300 or so megs started to go on empty. And God knew what else.

I was stuck. The clock had run out. The fantasy sweet-deal was over. I couldn't keep up the facade.

The clock. The god-damned clock. Do you know what the clock is, gentle reader? We'll get back to the story of me and my friend in just a little bit, but right now we need to talk about the clock. No, not the one on your desk or your wall or your frigging Win 98 32-bit desktop. THE clock. *The one that says you bought a piece of shit 9000.* Just like me.

Fifteen minutes after taking it home, the clock had run out. The clock of digital obsolescence. I hate that word—it has a clunky sound to it—but it's the only one that fits. Obsolescence. I had plunked down $2,000 for what I thought was a state-of-the-art gigantic party-animal silicon diode . . . and it turned out to be extinct 15 minutes after I brought it home. Think about that for a moment, will you? If you math nerds whip out your calculators, that comes damn, damn close to $133 a minute to use a computer that up and died on me 15 minutes later. A hundred and thirty-three dollars. Every minute. And that particular model had 15 minutes of real-time claim to being "state of the art." Then something else came along.

And I never even got it out of the box.

Oh, you forgot that part, didn't you my loyal reader . . . DJ and I hadn't even opened the box yet in our story. But why should we have? It was already years obsolete, even with the virgin factory seals in place and the hard drive untouched.

It's very much like radioactive decay; when you buy your lovely plastic box, it's really hot—oh lord is it hot! All packaged fancy and true. But by the time you get it to your car it's already reached half-life; half-dead already with all it's "newness" radiated away like so much magic dust. When you get it out of the box it's just as dead as a cold lump of iron. Dave Berry hit it right on the head when he said the computer stores should have trash cans right by the doors . . . so you can throw the computer away right after paying for it. You may as well follow his advice and save yourself some grief.

"I never really had a chance, did I?" DJ didn't answer; he could read everything I just typed above in my eyes. "They saw me coming. They see everybody coming. They. Them."

DJ nodded silently. He knew about "them", all right.

"You can't beat them, you know? They're too big. They're everywhere. They saw me and my two Gs, and the R&D boys at POS said, 'Oh boy, look at this kid with a little knowledge and a lot of money. We're gonna screw this kid and watch him smile while we're doing it.'"

DJ nodded again. He didn't have much to add. He didn't need to.

But later that day, after I had regained a little of my normal giddy, school-girl composure, he called me on the phone. By that time the POS 9000, what was left of it, was on my desk, plugged-in and alive in one sense of the word, but still just as dead as that lifeless lump of depleted uranium in every other sense.

DJ was saying on the other end of the phone, "Kiddo, everything you said was true. But you were wrong about one thing. Now I'm not going to repeat myself, so you'd better listen. There are some things they haven't seen. Fairly big things. So listen and take notes if you have to, because they don't want you to know a lot of this. Well, any of this. They like you weak. They like you small.

"Step into my office, kiddo, I wanna show you something . . ."

And I listened. And I took notes. And my heart lightened a little as he spoke. For the words he spoke were dark magic and mysteries beyond the things the R&D boys at POS computer company ever wanted you to know. Bad things. Wonderful things.

And, after a while, I started to smile.

CHAPTER ONE

DIGITAL AUDIO PIRACY

MPEG Layer 3 and Other Things That Go Bump in the Night

I WAS WATCHING THE IDIOT BOX the other day, just flipping through, when I chanced on *Entertainment Tonight*. Or maybe it was *Celebrity Stalkers* or *Worship Your Hollywood Gods*. Something like that. Halfway through the show, the blow-dried blonde clued me in to the fact that Celine Dion had recently purchased a wedding dress . . . a wedding dress that cost not a penny more or less than a quarter of a million dollars. A quarter of a million dollars. For a dress.

And here's another tidbit for the recycle bin: YOU paid for it. I know you did, so stop looking at me like that. You bought the *Titanic* CD or maybe just the CD single "It's All Coming Back To Me Now." Something by her charming, angelic, screeching voice . . . anything. And that money went directly from your wallet to her "Save the Wedding Dress" collection bin.

Doesn't feel too good to hear that, does it? Well, what would you say if I told you there was a way that hackers on the Internet download top-chart, full-length, CD-quality songs for *nothing*. You heard me: *no money*. They don't contribute to Celine Dion's wedding collection. They wouldn't if it meant their lives.

You don't believe me. I can tell. You think that I mean "midi" files. And you know what midi files are: 1) beneath contempt and 2) only used by high school students' web pages to be a little flashy. But, let me assure you, I do not mean midi files. Okay, so now you think I mean garbage quality snippets of real CD tracks for demo purposes . . . sort of the same deal you get with shareware games. Wrong! Let me say this again for the record: there is a way YOU, the average owner of a PC, can *illegally* download, play, and keep full-length, actual CD recordings by big-name groups and artists from Celine Dion to AC/DC to Metallica to Gordon Lightfoot. In some cases, full CD albums are easily within reach. (Yes, I am talking about 44 KHz, 16-bit sampling quality for those of you in the know . . .)

For the record:

Sampling rate—
8-bit: uses little drive space, results in noticeable gaps in recording
16-bit: uses huge amount of disk space; no gaps detectable in recording

Resolution—
11 KHz: low-level uses—telephony (answering machine) and some speech
22 KHz: mid-range uses—some music; recordings used for a short time
44 KHz: hi-end uses—CD-quality music (most everything of value)

These values may be mixed and matched, e.g., 16-bit 11 KHz is possible . . . but why? 8-bit works just as well for that use (telephony).

Before we proceed, take note: that "illegally" statement above was no misprint; it is ILLEGAL, as in AGAINST THE LAW to download *any* files on the Internet labeled ".mp3". You can and will be prosecuted. DO NOT DO IT. Remember, you bought this book to inform yourself about schemes and scams on the Internet perpetrated by criminals, not to join their ranks. Be warned.

So here's how to do it.

MP3 FILES

What we are talking about is, of course, MP3 files. When exploded that works out to Motion Pictures Expert Group Layer 3 compression technology. Egads! Did someone just sock you a good one in the gut? Nope, just call it MP3 for short. It's a file extension like any other. Check this out:

paris.jpg
test.doc
celine.mp3

Starting to come a little easier? Good. That ".xyz" is the file extension. It tells you and the computer what you're dealing with. Care to take a brief quiz? Okay, let's see how much you know already and go from there. The first one? Easy, "JPEG" or .jpg, it's a picture you can display on your browser or ACDSee or some other graphics viewer. It's just a way of compressing or shrinking an image down in a particular format. There are other formats for pictures, like ".gif" or ".pcx". You already knew that one, right?

And you know the next one, too. It's a text file. MS Word uses ".doc" to specify all text files. There are others: ".wps" for MS Works, ".rtf" for universal compatibility (rich text format). And, of course, we can't forget the lowly ".txt".

Now, the biggy— ".mp3". Again, that stands for "MPEG Layer 3." If you haven't used these files before (I will assume you have not), you probably don't have the proper software application to use one. Therefore, you can't open that type of file just yet, so don't click on it if you happen to have one. Your computer will chastise you harshly if you attempt to do so. I warned you. The exact (or "uncompressed") meaning of ".mp3" was given above, so let's examine it here in some detail. You need to have a clear picture of what we are talking about since this is the only file type this chapter will be concerned with. Motion pictures? How's that again? Yes, it's music recorded in "frames" exactly like a motion picture (see Fig. 6, p. 26). A typical song will have around 18,000 or so of those "frames" on which a portion of the digital signal is imprinted.

Next? "Layer 3 compression technology." That's a mouthful! What are we compressing? *A song.* Any old song your little heart desires. Step over here for a moment, will you? When you play a song on a compact disk player there is a digital readout. The average song is about three and a half minutes. Your computer probably has a CD-ROM drive built into it, and you probably have played an audio CD in it from time to time. Have you attempted to record a song from the CD onto the computer's hard disk? If you have not, please do so now. I will wait.

You there? Good. That means you have attempted that experiment or you know what I'm going to say next: you just consumed well over 36 megabytes (MB) of hard disk space. For one track. Problems! Don't worry, just delete the file and you've got that space back.

What would you say if there was a way to record that same track, at 44 KHz and 16-bit sampling (CD quality, in other words) with only 3 MB used? THREE. Trois. Trece. San. Drier. You'd call me screwy, wouldn't you? Well, you'd be wrong. Because there is such a way.

Let's go back to file extensions. That first recording you made was done in ".wav" format. It used 36 MB. The new method is ".mp3" which uses 3 MB. Did I just hear your head popping out of your ass? I did? Good. Then we're on the same wavelength, you and I.

Well (you're probably saying to yourself), I know *you* can do it Mr. Smartass Paladin Press writer computer nerd . . . but how do *I* do it? I'm going to tell you, if you'd just give me a moment of your precious life. Thank you.

This all goes back to the days of ".zip" file compression. For the sake of this book, I will assume that you know what a zipped or compressed file is, BUT I will refresh your memory (veterans can skip to the next paragraph). If you're REALLY lost then get on the Internet, go to Infoseek.com, and type in "file compression." For those who know a little but aren't sure, let's take you through it.

When you save a file it is in its "normal" or "uncompressed" mode. A dirt-common way to save hard-drive space (and download times) is to "compress" a file. This file is referred to as a "zipped" file, as in ".zip". Compressing results in about a third of the file being crunched together. For example, a 1 MB text file compressed is around 650 K. That's pretty good. Pictures (remember our friend and ally ".jpg"?) compress very poorly. Oh, you *can* do it, sure, but you're just wasting your time. Pictures have too much *nonredundant* information about them to compress. Text files have gobs of redundancy to play with, so you'll get terrific results.

. . . So things were good; everybody knew their respective places and stations in life, and nobody put up a fuss. Sure, some guys dreamed of compressing ".wav" files so they could fit entire albums on a hard drive, but nobody paid much attention to them. In fact, they were usually laughed at by small children and shunned if they talked about it too much outside of their computer labs.

And then, one day, some nerd in a white lab coat and filthy sneakers (think of Professor Frink from *The Simpsons* if that helps at all) came up with a brand new format (read: file extension). He called it MPEG. That allowed, as we have seen, mucho ".wav" format data to be crunched up neatly and reliably into a little package. They started off modestly with Layer 1 compression . . . which was an improvement over .wav but not much. Then Layer 2 came and ears pricked up sharply. Professor Frink was onto something, it seemed.

Then it all turned upside down. Layer 3 came along. Pretty soon those nerds started to be taken seriously by audiophiles. *Very* seriously. So seriously, in fact, that hundreds of FTP sites sprang up over night to catch the digital revolution (the one that will probably last 8.2 seconds in real-time). Thousands of CDs were converted over to MP3 format and posted for public use. A day of revolt against Celine Dion's wedding dress had arrived with hideous grandeur. As of this time, Celine still has no idea what's going on . . .

Is there any *legitimate* use for MP3? Not that I can see. Anything legitimate such as Windows sound effects may be stored most conveniently in .wav format. There would be no reason whatsoever to use MP3. It wouldn't work for sound effects regardless; you must use a special MP3 "player" (as discussed below) for anything to come out of the speakers with an MP3 file. Archiving CDs you already own is the most popular justification for MP3's existence.

But wait a minute. If you have the CD, which can never degrade in any fashion, what do you need MP3 copies for? You can't play them in your car (unless bloated back out onto .wav format) or in your home CD player. It's all horribly reminiscent of the AK-47 argument. You know how that one goes: you don't hunt with an AK, except the prey that goes on two legs and can read and write. So there's only one use for it. I don't agree with this, but the antigun nuts say it all the time. So the antigun nuts will say the same thing goes with MP3: you can't hunt with it and you can't target shoot with it; you can only kill people with it. And while I disagree vigorously with the AK-47 decision, I would be hard-pressed to make an argument for MP3. Sorry. That's just the way it is.

DIGITAL AUDIO TAPE

Remember DAT? It survived . . . but in a whole new underground sense of the concept. While *physical* DAT players sold zero units in the United States (and, brother, I mean ZERO), *virtual* DAT players (or "decks," as in "tape decks") are distributed freely on the Internet. Unlike in my previous book, I will *not* give any Web sites here for historical reasons. The readers of *The Ultimate Internet Terrorist* bitched and whined (and some even *called* me, much to their sorrow) that all the sites were down. Hence, I've decided to make you do the legwork yourself. That's the way it is, so you'd better learn to stand on your own two feet.

But I'm not cruel; I want to give you all the tools to get started. So here goes. Okay, first find a good *meta-search engine*. This is a specific kind of Web site that culls through many different *conventional search engines* for information (you of course provide the starting point).

Examples are (all on the WWW):

Dogpile.com
Cyber411.com
Metacrawler.com
Mamma.com

Now type in "WinAmp." This will result in many *Web sites* from which you may download the virtual DAT deck called "WinAmp." It is NOT illegal to download or operate WinAmp or any other virtual DAT deck/player (WinAmp, WinJey, etc.). It IS illegal to download and play/keep copyrighted ".mp3" files from record companies. Which is all of them, so DO NOT DO IT.

WinAmp is compatible with Windows 95 and 98 and *is* a professionally written program. It has gone through thorough beta testing and will not destroy or damage your computer in any way. It is unzipped (it's around 200 KB in its compressed state, so it's a quick download) and installed like any other program, either downloaded from the Web or store-bought. The great thing about WinAmp is that the "look" of the "face" can be modified rapidly and easily using "skins." Type in "WinAmp Skins" in Infoseek and see what comes up. Download them into the WinAmp/Skins directory and use Alt+S to change to a new "face" for your DAT deck. Some of my favorites include Pioneer, Technics, and Sony. As you can guess, these skins will transform WinAmp into a car-stereo-like look of those name brands. It's a lot better than the WinAmp skin out of the box, in any case; it's . . . pretty bad.

Using a mini-stereo jack from your line-out (or speakers) jack on the back of your computer, patch into your home stereo amplifier using RCA-type jacks purchased at a stereo supply store (see Fig. 5). The mini-to-RCA adapter is a *special item* that I purchased at Best Buy for $3. You must have the adapter to have any hope of true stereo sound. The item is not available at K-Mart or Wal-Mart; I don't know why, it just isn't. Now, don't let me lead you astray, you *can* use your computer's speakers or buy a pair of Yamaha amplified computer speakers and save yourself the hassle if you don't have a regular home stereo. But remember, the .mp3 files available on the Internet are TRUE CD quality top-charters that you *will* want to listen to through your big speakers. The adapter cord gets the sound from the computer to those big speakers; that's all. And, no, there's no "easy way." Ask me in e-mail for an "easy way" and pay the consequences!

GETTING YOUR FIRST MP3

Okay, you've downloaded WinAmp, along with a Sony skin to make it look like something better than dirt-shit, and patched your line-out from your sound card to the stereo system in your dorm room. Good. You're just about ready to blast "Ghetto Superstar" to that math nerd asshole across the hall. Almost, I said—slow down, hoss. We need to get some of those .mp3 files to play on that DAT deck. It's just like the survival fire triangle: fuel, oxygen, and the vital spark. Well, we have computer, the software . . . now we need a bone for it all to chew on.

Can you type in "ghettokillaz.mp3" under Infoseek and laugh while it's downloading? NO. It's not that easy by a long chalk. You have to use an *indirect method* of obtaining worthwhile .mp3 files.

You *must* do the following:

1) Go to Infoseek or any other search engine.
2) Type in "MP3 Search Engines".
3) Go to *any listed* site there (such as MediaFind).
4) Type in the name of the song you want (in MediaFind's site, for example).
5) Click "search."
6) Obtain the FTP site number (as in ftp://123.45.678.9).
7) Start CuteFTP and "quick connect" to that ftp:// site.
8) Download the .mp3 by clicking twice on the song title.

Don't worry, we'll go over the stuff about FTP in a later chapter ("Tools of the Trade"). The MP3 file will transfer automatically . . . but transfer times are SLOW. You can and will get a "fast" time of 30 minutes for a 3.5 to 4 meg long file. And usually a lot longer. *Realistic* connection rates (not what some kid who wants to sell you a computer will tell you) with a modem are around 2.8 KBs. And that's on a good day. A very good day.

You *cannot* download MP3 files from the World Wide Web using Netscape Navigator, MicroSucks Internet Explorer, or any other civilian-type browser. IT WILL NOT WORK, FOLKS. Why? Simple: because MP3 files are not stored on the World Wide Web! They are on the Internet, just not on the Web. The terms are *not* synonymous. Examine Figure 4 on page 17 in some detail. Soak it in. Become one with Figure 4. Learn to love it. Make it your best friend, your companion in life. Later, consider marrying it and starting a fam—

Okay, I'm being a little sarcastic, but you need to understand that the Internet is a very general thing, and the WWW is a very specific thing. The WWW is just a part of the Internet. File Transfer Protocol (FTP) sites are another. And so on. Without this knowledge you will never survive in this electronic war zone. The natives will club you and make you their bitch. You will never bask in the glory of having 1.2 gigs of .mp3 files for FREE. So study up!

"But" (you may say), "I read ahead, went to Infoseek.com and typed in 'ghettokillaz.mp3.' From there (skipping steps 2 through 8) I found 'Jimmy's Lair of Sodomy, Warez, and MP3Z' on the Web. Jimmy (the sodomite) had *tons* of Web links to those same songs we all hear on the radio when I clicked on 'MP3 Archives' in his Web site. So who's chain are you pulling there, Huxstable?"

Well, you cold-cocked me, that's for sure. You *can* sometimes find working Web links to some songs you may wish to possess. But 1) the songs are almost always "bargain binners" at best, 2) the quality is garbage, and 3) the links are *almost always* dead. I can not stress this enough: if you want real music, you must use the steps listed above. Having said that, let's guide you graphically on a successful journey to getting you that first .mp3 file . . .

SEARCHING FOR "celine dion"

IP Address	Port	Logon	Password	Last Checked	Ratio	Site Speed
1) 24.112.4.194	21	mp3	mp3	02-03 at 12:58	None	[»»»»»]
2) 114.20.94.1	45	anonymous	e-mail	02-03 at 12:58	1:10	[»»]

Figure 1. A sample MP3 search query result. Note the different port addresses you must use to connect to the site. "Site speed" is a simple way to tell if "1" or "2" would be the better choice. "Ratio" is used to let you know the site expects something in return.

Search results for jackson   (Returned 1–100 of 147 entries after 36.475 seconds.)

12.6.116.219 , Port: 1313, Login: gimme, Password: mp3s, Files: 806
Site name: Phantom Ryu s FTP
server last checked: Jan 7 , NoT: n.a.

Path : /pub/80's/
1) Michael Jackson - Bad.mp3   [3.965.173]
2) Michael Jackson - Man in the Mirror.mp3 [5.119.554]

This site seems to be a RATIO site
128.100.192.52 , Port: 21, Login: mp3, Password: mp3, Files: 408
Site name: Mael s FTP , Siteinfo: 8:00 - 1:00 daily
server last checked: Thu Jan 7 23:44:35 1999 , NoT: n.a.

Path : /Mp3/Old School/
3) Michael Jackson - Billy Jean.mp3   [4.620.402]

Figure 2. Another version of an MP3 search. This is a more detailed and useful list. The "path" denotes the location of the file. Ratio sites are clearly marked as such.

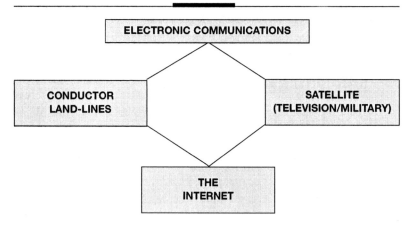

Figure 3. The Internet—a highly abbreviated schematic to all its infernal intricacies.

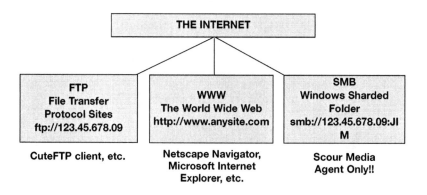

Figure 4. This shows us that the Internet, far from being one thing unto itself (like a slab of marble), is actually composed of many smaller parts (like a car). FTP sites are of major importance to Chapter 1. FTP sites can't be accessed using your browser. They can only be accessed using an FTP client application such as CuteFTP or WS-FTP. Also, SMB sites require a special software pack called Scour Media Agent. It's available at Scour.net. Don't ask!

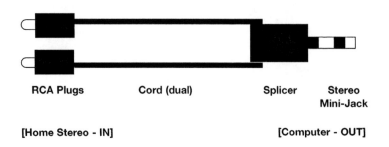

RCA Plugs   Cord (dual)   Splicer   Stereo
Mini-Jack

[Home Stereo - IN]   [Computer - OUT]

Figure 5. The soon-to-be-banned stereo RCA-to-mini jack adapter. This baby gets the signal from the computer to your stereo system. Computers come with shitty speakers, so you'll want to pick one of these up. This adapter can ONLY be found at specialty stereo shops as of this time (it's only $3). Try Best Buy but forget WalMart. Set your stereo to any blank input device; DAT is of course the preferred input, but PHONO works just as well (although not as aesthetically pure). Sooner or later the feds will wise up and ban this device . . . right along with high-capacity handgun magazines, AK-47s, and puncture-resistant tires, so get yours today!

STORAGE SOLUTIONS

While MP3 files take up comparatively little space, they do take up *something* for their existence. This amounts to 3 to 5 megabytes of memory on your computer's internal (hard) disk drive (HDD) per file/song. And, if you're like me, you'll say, "Big deal! I'll eat up all the mp3 you can give me; I just bought a new computer with a 3.2 gig hard drive! Ha! I spit on your mother's grave!" Well, OK, you can get away with that attitude for a while . . . and then you'll start to eat those words. You'll go to bed one night with the stars and the moon in the respective place in the heavens and everything dorky . . . and then . . . oh, and then. Then you'll wake up and find 210 MB free disk space left, and then where will you be? Sending me e-mail and condemning me?

Probably. But that won't help. What you need is *external storage.* May I elaborate? Thank you. External storage is something outside your computer that holds a massive amount of files (files, data, computer information . . . it's all the same sweet stuff). This, obviously, frees up your internal disk for more important, everyday things like word processing, calendars, spread sheets, accounting software, crap like that.

Okay, so you need something external . . . but what? There's a huge menu out there, as you know already if you've owned a computer for any length of time or investigated this part of the computer age at all.

You may choose from:

Zip Drive	= 100 MB/disk	$ 50
The LS Super Disk	= 120 MB/disk	$ 50
CD Rewritable (CD-RW)	= 650 MB/disk	$300
SyQuest	= 1.00 GB/disk	$300
Jaz Drive	= 2.00 GB/disk	$500
* New Hard Drive	= 6.50 GB/disk	$200

Sheew! Where to even begin? Well, I suppose I could just tell you right off the bat that your best all-around choice would be–in my opinion–CD-RW. It holds an ungodly amount of MP3 files, is rewritable (hence the RW), and the disks them-selves cost less than any of the other media types listed above. It's also CD-ROM-compatible. You may play these disks in your existing CD-ROM or on a stereo CD player (if in .wav for-mat). You will almost certainly find an existing empty drive bay on your computer where you may insert the dear thing, BUT ALWAYS LEAVE YOUR EXISTING CD-ROM IN PLACE. These CD-RW units are slow; typical read times are 6x. Your original CD-ROM is probably 20x or even 32x. Leave it in and use the CD-RW for recording only. Also, CD has no magnetic signature; leaving it on a stereo won't erase it. Temperatures won't fry it and static discharge from fingers won't scramble it. Once it's on a CD, brother, it's on there to stay!

Second best? (L)aser(S)ervo-Super Disk. It's cheap, fast (connects to the hard-drive cable inside your computer), and may be either internal, replacing the original floppy drive, or external, connecting to the printer (parallel) port. You'll lose some speed with a parallel port connect, but not much. Nevertheless, best to rip out your old floppy and replace it with the Super Disk. Of course, LS can and does read old-style floppy disks perfectly every time with no modifications.

In the "gray area" we have the SyQuest and Jaz series of drives. The media (individual disks that you must purchase) are outrageously expensive . . . some even in the hundreds of dollars for a single disk. EEEEEGGGGAADDDSS! But they hold gigs of space, not megs, and are faster (nearly IDE hard drive speed) than CD-RW. They are twice as fast and hold twice as much as CD-RW, just so you can keep score. But the money! Oh my God, the money you'll spend! Also, what if a Jaz disk dies on you? You'll lose a gig of data and replace it with a $99 disk. Wow, talk about a mistake! These are always external drives, so you won't have to open the computer to use them, which for some folks is a major concern since computer techs will FUCK YOU TO DEATH to install a simple CD-RW drive.

Last on the list is the low and pissed-on Zip drive from Iomega. Yes, these are cheap and hold a fair chunk of your life, BUT the LS Super does it faster and better . . . and, per media, cheaper to boot! I'd say the conventional Zip is a thing of the past. You'd have to be crazy to buy it in the face of LS or CD-RW. But I'm not you, am I? Research it yourself and find out what you'd be happiest with.

To summarize, CD-RW is the best value and best quality (and nonmagnetic, so it's super safe as well) followed by LS Super Disk, which is the exact same size as the conventional floppy disk but holds 120 MB of info and has hard-drive speed.

But here's another method: just buy a separate hard drive. Excuse me but isn't that a little expensive? No way! It used to be just a few years ago, but in today's world a new HDD is between $150 and $250. That's it. So buy a second hard drive, put it alongside your original one (yes, leave that one in), and make frequent "mirrors" of your original HDD. Only buy a HDD that has ultra-DMA (equates to superfast data transfer times) and at least 6.0 GB. All brands are about the same in terms of track record (reliability), so I don't care what anyone says; buy the cheapest one you can get from c-net shopper.com (explained in "Tools of the Trade"). Seagate, Western Digital, and JTS are all fine. You gain a lot from this method: it's cheap, quick, and requires no external disks to swap (read: lose) or purchase. For the price, space is looney-tunes good (6 gigs goes a helluva long way), and you won't have yet another "black box" sitting on your desk. But, baby, if it goes bad it REALLY goes bad, and you will have no recourse to save yourself from utter data hell. Be warned.

MEDIA AGENTS

Yep, the Media Agents are coming to get ya! Remember that Fig. 4 we were supposed to fall in love with? Please refresh your RAM by referring to that diagram now. See that "SMB" on the far right? Well, that's a special case. These are MP3 files tucked away—hidden away, actually—on something called "Windows Shared Folders." This is like FTP but it's private. It's a private membership belonging to Scour.net (on the http:// side of things, of course), which you may access by typing in www.scour.net and letting the page load (takes forever). You must download their special software called "Scour Media Agent" or SMA for short. Do not confuse this with smb:// since these are separate things. SMA is software; smb:// is a protocol. Like I said, don't ask, I'm just as lost as you are. Their Web site (Scour.net) will show you how to download the Scour Media Agent program. It is no harder than getting your dirty little hands on CuteFTP. Same deal. Download and install it.

You may access these special "smb://" sites by going to the Web site "Scour.net" in your Netscape or MS browser. Scour.net is a search engine for MP3 files, but it will return mostly those smb:// type sites. A "normal" MP3 search engine, such as MediaFind, will *not* return matches containing smb:// sites. MediaFind will exclusively return ftp:// sites, which you may access with CuteFTP or something similar (see "Tools of the Trade" elsewhere in this book).

Once in Scour.net, simply type in a song title and hit

"search." A new screen will appear with any matches (usually multiple matches will return). Assuming you have already downloaded the Scour Media Agent software application, you may now click directly on the resulting hot links (underlined and in red) from Scour.net's web site. This will download the MP3 file onto your computer. Please note, however, that *many* hot links from Scour.net are useless at certain times of the day. This is a general phenomenon that you will find using CuteFTP as well. Servers (such as ftp:// or smb://) are operated on a time-sharing basis, meaning they are only "on" at certain times of the day. As of this writing, it's still very much a guessing game as to when, exactly, any one particular server's time-share window is currently "open." And that means you'll have to do some intelligent fishing at certain times of the day (morning, afternoon, night) to find when the damn thing is taking orders. However (and this is why I added the coda "as of this writing"), things are getting better; the current trend on MediaFind is to update server hits by the hour, which means only the *currently available* servers will show up as successful matches to your search request. Makes things just a little easier, eh?

Scour.net is a great place to hang out . . . and you may expect the occasional miracle. I said occasional, not always, so don't get your hopes up. I have friends (ahem) who have found really old, neglected hits like "Hip to be Square" by Huey Lewis & The News on Scour.net. It is not without its charms. I would stick with MediaFind (ftp://) for my day-to-day explorations for common 80s and 90s hits, but Scour.net will get you out of many a jam through its secret organization of smb:// sites. These, again, are exclusive to Scour.net's site, so it is very much worth your "second best" choice for MP3 downloads. Also, Scour.net is much easier to use than ftp site search engines (remember, like MediaFind). All you do is click on the red link and it gets the file. No running for CuteFTP, typing in the nonsense, waiting forever for it to log you in, and searching through mazes and corridors of directories and sub-sub-sub directories to get your goodies. Like I said, use it, baby, use it!

. . . that is until the feds come to your door and say, "Um, excuse us, sir, but do you *like* infringing on Celine Dion's right to a quarter-of-a-million-dollar wedding dress?" And then, WHAM! They slap the love bracelets on you . . .

Heh heh heh.

ODDS AND ENDS

First we need to talk about some of the finer points of proper search etiquette for MP3 files. You need to understand that people on the 'net who operate FTP sites often have very low literary skills. And that leads to many failed searches. Would you believe I even found a reference to Belinda Carlisle as "lady-carl"? Can you imagine the level of downright stupidity it takes to list a group of songs under a bullshit name like that? I spent untold *hours* looking for the woman's 80s classic "Mad About You" and came up empty. Then, on a lark, I typed in a portion of the last name: "carl". It came right up. Man, that was scary!

Now, for example, say you're searching for "Elton John–Sad Songs (Say So Much)." Where to begin? Probably the best way is to type in "Elton" in an MP3 search engine page and scroll through (see the MediaFind screen shot above on a successful search) the matches. Another *good* way is to type in something distinctive about the title, such as "sad." A *bad* way is to type in the entire song title; bad for this case since the title is so long. Another poor way is to type in "song," since this will yield thousands of bogus matches that have nothing to do with Elton John.

Such a song may be listed on many different FTPs as:

eltonj – ssongs
john, e – sadsongs(say)
unknown – sadsong
songs(say so much)
elton – sad

That's pretty wild! You'd *never* find that particular song trying to use the exact title. Not in a million. But using the artist name works a lot better. (I purposefully skewed the title to make a point: people on the 'net can't spell, so don't expect exact matches.)

Next the topic usually turns to RATIO sites. What the hell? Did someone blow gas? You may think so if you don't check "Ignore RATIO servers" on the MediaFind/MP3 search engine. Ratio sites or just "ratios" are a pain in the ass. They have TONS of great MP3, but you have to upload in order to download. It's really not that much of a pain . . . especially if you really need that one MP3 you just can't find on the "leech" sites. To upload, just highlight a file of yours (preferably an MP3 you just downloaded somewhere else) and click on the toolbar tag with the "up arrow." Simple enough, right? But you have to wait while the entire file goes through. You can–and people do it all the time–just cut off the download once your *ratio has been met*. For instance, if a certain RATIO site insists on a 1:3 trade, you need to upload 1 MB to download 3 MB. Usually MP3 files are at least 3 MB long, resulting in a credit on your end of 9 MB, which you may download from the RATIO site. Do you follow me? Read it again. I'll wait.

But say you don't need 9 MB. You just need 6 MB for a really long rendition of "ghettokillamotherfuckerz.mp3." You may simply elect to stop the upload by clicking on CuteFTP's *stop sign* located on the uppermost right of the screen. This results in a credit to your account, which the FTP server will calculate from the time you clicked on the stop sign. You may then simply get what you came for in the usual way (as long as it doesn't exceed 6 MB, as in this example). Needless to say FTP operators don't like this. And, yes, they *will* come for your ass. They log all IPs and will hunt you down for giving them a useless upload. So don't do it, kids, or I should say don't *over-do* it. Sometimes they'll let it slide once or twice, but if you make a career of it they will get you. Count on it.

Now, some legal questions. How on earth do these FTP sites stay open for more than 15 minutes? You'd think Janet Reno would shut them down in a heartbeat. Well, they use a legal loophole, of course: they tell anyone who asks that they legally own the original CD (remember the AK-47 argument above). And they are prepared to prove it. Record companies *do* allow you to make archival copies *if* you own the original recording. So FTP owners are halfway out the woods. But FTP site operators *post* these archival (and very legal) copies on the 'net. Is that a problem? You may think so, since FTPs are open to the public, but attend: if you *legally* own something, how can anyone tell you what to do with it? If you own a painting, paid for it fair and square, and want to put it in your front yard, will anyone stop you? Nope. If you, further, put a sign alongside the work in plain view that invites anyone to stop over for a look-see, will the feds stop you? No way. But–*if someone steals the painting they'll come for the thief, not the owner.* Get my drift? And that's why it's *your* ass on the line, not the FTP site owner.

Take heed, O surfer of the Internet, take you heed . . .

The cats who operate these sites are a nervy lot. They're bold . . . as Stephen King wrote, "Rats sometimes grow bold in the dark . . ." They sure do. Sooner or later the feds will close it all down, but in the here-and-now, man, these cats are brazen. They operate in loosely connected "rings" and, more often than not, have close ties to the underground or "Darkside" of the 'net. When you're in an FTP site that specializes in MP3, you'll usually notice other "folders" (a la Windows Explorer) that have titles like "warez" or "crackz," and, as explained elsewhere in this book, these are the forbidden files associated with cyber-criminals operating like a low-level e-mafia on today's 'net. Sound strong? Read *The Ultimate Internet Terrorist* and tell me what you think.

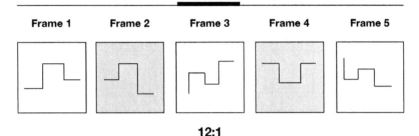

12:1

Figure 6. MPEG layer 3 compression of an audio signal into digital format.

What we're seeing here is how the computer encodes or compresses an analog (.wav) song into an MP3 digital signal. The result is a series of "frames" or snapshots that allow precise control over the recording. The term "Motion Picture Expert Group" is derived from this system of using still-frames to record the music. That nice, flat, continuous line is a graphical rendition of the digital signal; it's not a wave form. The figure "12:1" is the ratio of compression. Don't confuse this ratio with RATIO FTP sites. That's a variable ratio set by the operator himself. This ratio is a fixed deal. It's 1 byte of MP3 for every 12 bytes of analog signal (.wav). That's what allows you to get a 36 MB file into 3 MB. Gotta admit, those computer nerds have their uses!

CHAPTER TWO

TOOLS OF THE TRADE

Secrets Bill Gates and Janet Reno Never Told You About

MOST OF US THINK THE INTERNET (see Fig. 4) is confined to the World Wide Web (WWW). And that Netscape (or Bill Gates' horrifying example of science gone mad, Internet Explorer) will see us through thick and thin, never letting us down, never complaining, never buckling under the pressure of revolution after revolution on the Internet. The Immortal Web Browser will handle anything short of a nuclear blast. Well, sweet hearts and sugar cookies, you're wrong. It's hit a bump in the road. The mother of all bumps in the road.

Meet FTP. It stands for *File Transfer Protocol.* Protocols are just rules or conventions; don't let that scare you. For example, a *protocol* for the English language is that most ordinary written statements shall end with a period. That's a rule we all agree to. *Interrogatories* end with a question mark; they're not statements and therefore follow a different protocol. Get it? *Demands* end with exclamation points. So listen closely!

The WWW has a protocol called "http://" which stands for "hyper text transport protocol" and that's good for a lot of things like making Web pages you can interact with. But it takes a *lot* of resources to make a Web page interactive (http://). College students, researchers for government agencies, and others who just want to provide files or other resources at minimal cost and coding (slang for programming a Web page) need an alternative; they don't need or want flashy Web pages with Java scripting. And that's why there are alternatives to being on the WWW (see Fig. 3). Think about this: you could drive a car to work, take the bus, or just walk. The WWW is driving. FTP is walking. SMB is the bus. FTP doesn't require a lot of special HTML coding that a Web page does; it's more like a simple computer-to-computer connection without all the fuss. That's why a typical FTP screen looks like Windows File Manager (remember that?) or Windows Explorer (see Fig. 7).

But you need a special program to access this "other side" of the Internet. They're called, simply, "FTP clients." You may search for the most popular one, CuteFTP, by using a search engine like HotBot. Download the one you want (Win 95, Win 3.x, etc.), and then execute as normal . . . which in today's

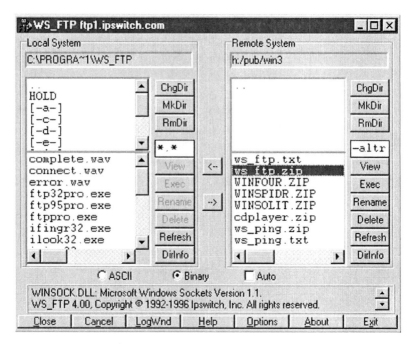

Figure 7. A File Transfer Protocol interface. Note how similar it is to Windows applications you use already.

world means running the included install program. Simple
enough, right? Some other names of popular *FTP clients*
include: WS-FTP (what all the hackers use in college) and
BulletProof FTP. BulletProof FTP is an actual browser for
FTP sites and may be used with the ease of Navigator, which
you are accustomed to. But remember, an FTP client is a dis-
tinct *software application* from Netscape Navigator (a WWW
browser); they're two different programs.

Logging into FTP "War Dialers" is an art unto itself. Oh,
yes, I too was once naive enough to think that once you'd located a hot FTP site, all you'd have to do is follow the site's own
login procedures to the letter and . . . presto! You would be in.
Wrong! Oh, Lord, I can't tell you how frustrating it is to simply
login to these FTP sites! An MP3 search engine (such as
MediaFind) will pass on to you what each particular site uses
for usernames and passwords.

Some common ones are:

login / password
mp3 / mp3
iso / iso
iwant / mp3z
gimme / mp3z
leech / mp3z

And there are many others impossible to catalog. But you
know what? It's usually all bad information . . . given by the server itself! Why? Some grand conspiracy involving Janet Reno and
Señor Gates in some plot to take over the universe? Will you dial
and redial until your death certificate is signed for you? Hardly.
The veterans among you will know what it really is: sheer
incompetence. Yes, that old demon from beyond time is here at
work again. I spoke of it briefly in *The Ultimate Internet Terrorist*;
it's something ubiquitous on all facets of the 'net. It's everywhere. You see, the happy-time folks who run these FTPs often
change their logins and passwords for security reasons, which is
bright of them, but they forget to tell you about it! Specifically,

they don't report it in their info which is forwarded to the search engines (Media Find), which of course is where you get your info from. Why do they do this? Some just don't give a damn; they're in college and could care less. Others honestly forget or, in the same vein, mean to but something always comes up . . .

Can we beat this problem? Yep, sure can. Try using any and all *combinations* of the login/passes I listed above. Make your own list from MP3 search expeditions. Mix and match until a successful "hit" happens. This means you'll have to go against this site's own advice for what it wants. But this is not a problem; it isn't illegal to type in common logins to get a system to respond. Isn't this hacking? Well, you got me–it is . . . but of a very *limited* variety. Remember, these sites are designed with the full and explicit knowledge that the general public has total access to their "directories" (as illustrated elsewhere), and that they *want* said public to enter their site. You'd be surprised at the number of sites which will say they need "mp3 / mp3" to enter when you can most always use "anonymous login" to make it in! Ironic, no? *Anonymous login* is accomplished by merely checking the circle (in the FTP software you should have by now) for, you guessed it, anonymous login.

Sometimes FTP sites will tell you in the *login screen* (in CuteFTP or otherwise) that you need to visit their *Web* site for download access. This is perfectly reasonable. And safe. This request is *not* an ambush, just an advertising attempt. They will, generally, give you an addy such as: http:quik.shot.org/~mikiesmp3. You need to go back to your Web browser to enter that site. Once there, you will find further directions. You could be asked to click on the "Teen Face Fuckers" (or other equally ridiculous and lame ad) *banner* button and find a login and password in that site. Something such as "visa" and "accepted" could be logins and passes, respectively; the Web site will tell you what to look for. Be warned: at times these sites can be downright insulting, demanding that you type in "ima" for login and "stupidleech" for password. Such a site is a waste and should be *nuked* as discussed in "Information Security" (search for WinNuke under HotBot).

In the same arena, avoid FTP sites that threaten you in the

so-called "welcome message" screen. By "threat" I mean statements such as:

SEVENTEEN LEECH FUCKS ALREADY BANNED. ARE YOU NEXT? THINK IT OVER AND DON'T FUCK WITH US. DON'T EVEN THINK OF UPLOADING ANYTHING NOT ON OUR REQUEST LIST OR BE KICKED.
ALL IP ACTIVITY LOGGED. ONE LOG-IN PER IP. NO EXCEPTIONS. FUCK WITH US AND DIE.

See what I mean? Not something that makes you feel right at home, is it? Believe me, kids, there are plenty of good MP3 sites out there. Don't take any shit. A "good" site is one in which the automated FTP welcome screen says something like:

Hi! Welcome to Jimmyz Mp3 Site Devoted to Celine Dion and other Top 10 singles. Please feel free to download what you want and if you have a fast connection please upload something to contribute to this site. Thanks for dropping by!

Wow! What a difference simple courtesy makes! On today's Internet that level of decency is a rare thing to find. Always support such sites by "uping" a few good files and remember to drop a "thank you" e-mail if the connections are decent.

After jumping through their often frustrating (and sometimes incorrect) hoops, you can go back to CuteFTP and enter the login (username) and password. That should let you in. If it doesn't work, try another site entirely; you're just wasting time from that point on.

TELEPHONY

Yes. The humble and oft-misunderstood telephone. But brought to a hideous new life in today's ugly world of technology-driven crime. You've probably heard the craze: talk to your loving mistress using your computer and an ISP connection (an Internet on-ramp such as earthlink.net, etc.) for free. Well, you know, nothing is free, but you can come damn close. You have to buy a computer–make sure it has telephony support (a modem that acts like a comms center; see the "Aggressive E-mail" section elsewhere in this book)–and a microphone. Then you need to get an ISP account. Oh, and did I forget to tell you that you need to make sure *everybody* you call has those same things? Did I? Sorry. It's my advanced age: makes thinking difficult.

Psst. Come here. Yeah, you. There's something else I "forgot" to tell you: what I said above? Yeah, it's all bullshit. You *can* and will be talking long-distance to anyone you wish for FREE without a computer. And those people you call? They don't need a computer either. Interested? Good.

It's called APLIO phone. That's the brand name for this magic black box under discussion (it really is a black box). It retails for $200. Each. Yep, you've got to have one of these gadzoodies *for everyone you call*, and they must have an ISP account as you must. Sorry, there's no way around it. That's just life. So where's the deal? You don't need a computer on either end. But, since you own one already, you may hook up the APLIO phone externally on the same phone line. You may buy one for your closest friends (those with or without computers) and call them day and night, for months at a time without incurring a single long-distance charge. And there are tricks you can use to smooth the process along. If you've ever used "NetPhone" or something similar, you know that you and the person you're calling need to be on the 'net at the same time. To coordinate this, you usually call the person conventionally and say, "I'm on," and then hang up. That's OK, but it still results in your being charged (by the minute, as you know). A solution? Use 1-800-COLLECT or a similar service to leave a message for the person. You say something to the effect of, "It's Jason on the Alpio. The time is 1:20 P.M." Now if the person is home, he gets the call, the message is played, and he simply declines to accept the call. But your message is received all the same. So he gets on his ISP and calls you back on Alpio or NetPhone or what-

ever. It's an old, old dodge, I mean it's literally been around forever, but it works real well.

SHOPAHOLICS ANONYMOUS

Well . . . not anonymous but shopaholics . . . YES! Want a
BAD way to purchase a new Ultra-DMA Seagate drive? Go to
Best Buy or Computer City (gag!). There you will be directed
to a product you know nothing about and don't really want to
buy. Afterwards, the store will harass you and your family for
MONTHS via telephone for extended warranty coverage you
neither need nor want. Nice, huh? All for a full retail price you
will vomit over after you read this section. (Reread the
Introduction to recall what I went through buying a new computer if you want a good horror story.)

Want a GOOD way to buy a new Ultra-DMA Seagate
drive? Use the WWW. Namely, go to www.shopper.com or
wherever c-net shopper.com is at when you read this and buy,
buy, buy! Why am I so adamant? Because, you see, I'm a loyal
customer. Have been for years. C-net shopper.com is a vast *network* of companies that deal exclusively via Internet for their
clientele. They are not crooks or hucksters in any way. You will
receive your product in a matter if two to three days for the
usual UPS shipping rate. Example? I'm currently typing this
with a PC Concepts Wave 2000 keyboard, which retails (again,
as of this writing) for nearly $90. I found it in c-net shopper's
network from a company called "Techwave" for $29. With free
shipping. I received the *brand new* device within one working
day (not counting ordering or receiving days). Man, talk about
service! Yes, they were very happy to take my money, but so
were the assholes at Computer City, which 1) did *not* carry that
model and 2) charged full retail for similar products, many
times what I paid (AND would have harassed me via telephone
for days afterwards with their special extended warranty . . .)
On average, expect to pay around 40 percent of what you would
pay via retail stores or "factory outlets" or whatever they're calling their scams these days. *Forty percent.* That's not peanuts,

folks, that's nearly half off everything. Seagates? Around $250 retail. Get the same thing via this method for $150. I'm serious as a heart attack with wings and afterburners.

In *The Ultimate Internet Terrorist* I warned readers about the horrors of shopping on-line. But this is not *ordering* on-line. These companies have telephones that are hot. Use them. Do not give your credit card over the WWW. Guerrilla warfare rules *still apply*, as we talked about in *The Ultimate Internet Terrorist*.

VIDEO GAMES

Do you like the idea of being able to play Pole Position, Millipede, and Gyruss right on your home PC for free? No? Then skip this section . . . it's for hard-core gamers from the '80s only! And I mean the '80s, too. Not the '70s, not the '90s, and certainly not the frigging year 2000. I mean true '80s retro-arcade classics–everything from Ms. PacMan to Stargate and all the way up to Outrun. How to do it? Use a search engine and look around for "arcade emulation sites." These will specialize in near-professionally written programs that will magically metamorphose your PC into those arcade beasts of the '80s. I say "near-professionally" since you may get a real buggy emulator from time to time and, while it's not harmful to you or your computer, may lock up your current Windows session so badly you'll have to unplug the thing. You can find the ancient Commodore 64, 128, and Amiga emulators, Atari 2600 (the home gaming system), 400/800 and ST. Coleco and Intellivision are a stone's throw away. Game images are also easily available . . . although most are unbelievably crappy when seen 20 years later.

Currently there is a program called "MAME" (Multiple Arcade Machine Emulator) which, unlike the ones I described above, is an *exact replica* of the arcade classics mentioned elsewhere. This means that you will be playing—I can't stress this enough—*the exact coin-op arcade machine* in your home, not a translation. The cost? Nothing.

Hey . . . isn't this a little ILLEGAL? Yes, it is. Next question. But take heart. There are so many hundreds of thousands of people downloading the same programs that it would be well nigh impossible for them to find you. Using a proxy server, it *is* (almost) impossible for them to find you (as detailed elsewhere).

MAME is just an executable program; by itself it is nonfunctional. You must download ROM images of stolen games for it to work. As you already guessed, these are available in mass quantities (again, as of this time) by searching for "rom archives & mame." These come individually zipped (gyruss.zip, etc.) and are from 10K to 200K zipped. Pretty reasonable.

MAME must be *unzipped* (decompressed) and placed in a directory, as must the ROMS (in a subdirectory called ROMS). You must read all documentation for it yourself, as no one will help you run these buggers; it's just too risky for people to stick their necks out and stand up for a newbie. For all they know, you're a cop gathering evidence for THE BUST (the one that will shut down the emulation scene for good in a few years).

Also, I recommend you use *only* the DOS versions of any and all emulators procured from the Internet underground. The reason is that, while these kids can write some decent code, they just don't have the resources to thoroughly *beta test* their stuff under a tricky OS (operating system) like Windows 95/98. DOS is a different story. DOS is "clean"; there's not a lot to worry about from a programmer's point of view. But Windows does a lot of funky things. Ever notice how *file sizes* are different under Windows and DOS? Try it; I think you'll be not-so-pleasantly amused. Just click on *MS-DOS shortcut* and examine a certain *directory's* size, now do the same thing with Windows Explorer. Hmmmm . . . someone's wrong, somewhere!

Anywho, you *will* see a lot of emulators (often shortened on a WWW site to "emus") advertised as being 100-percent compatible with Windows . . . but don't trust them; the programmers are just showing off for their girlfriends or talking tough to intimidate others. Use DOS and save a reboot or two. Or three.

Incidentally, the current rumor is that Micro$ucks is planning to, um, "acquire" MAME and sell it for hundreds of dollars to an unsuspecting and ignorant public . . . just the way they "acquired" and ruined HotMail.com. But *you* won't let that happen . . . will you?

WAREZ–THE EVIL REVISITED

In *The Ultimate Internet Terrorist*, I wrote about the phenomenon of "warez." Warez is one of those cute "Darkside" words so vital to the lexicon of hackerdom. Hackers use this darkside slang to identify themselves to others in the know (as in a chatroom). It's much like the medieval code languages of thieves. Warez refers to the very general realm of illegally duplicated software. In *The Ultimate Internet Terrorist*, I accurately reported that warez were, by and large, a blind alley with only a few "good" links on the entire WWW. Well, that was then and this is now. Warez have really exploded since I wrote *The Ultimate Internet Terrorist*, and here I want to explore this darkest of Darksides a little further. . . .

What do warez consist of? Hell, all the hot titles are here from Micro$oft's entire product line to the latest games (top sellers, too, not just emulated '80s crap). Other slang includes "crackz," "appz," and "gamez," which we will explore in turn.

CRACKZ

Crackz refers to a small (and obviously noncommercial) program that will prevent a demo version of a major title like Norton Anti-Virus from locking up and becoming useless after a certain time (usually 30 days). You can "crack" the program open (as a safe is cracked). Crackz may be specific (such as @Guard_Crack.zip, the title of a well-known Internet security program) or very general, such as what's commonly known as a "date cracker." "Date" crackers will attempt to break *any* program that locks up after the trial month is due. This is a 50-50 shot. It does *not* work often enough for me to recommend it, but give it a shot anyway; don't let me push you around.

The generally accepted method of *cracking* software is to

first locate the *commercial download program* you want from a site on the Web. This may be a huge distribution site of demos such as www.softseek.com, or it could be the specific manufacturer's site. For instance, if someone wanted "Norton's Anti-Virus," he or she could simply type it in HotBot and jump to the company's homepage (www.symantec.com). Next, he would simply opt to download the "30-day trial version." That's what we mean (in brief) when we say "getting the demo." What good is a demo? Demos, you see, are 100-percent full versions of the real, honest-to-God store-bought programs that just "happen" to have a time limit embedded in the code. Such demos expire (see above) and demand to be deleted from your system (they will refuse to work regardless after expiring). But if we could junk out the time limit somehow . . . why, we could save upwards of several thousand dollars on software from Worst Buy, could we not? Beyond that, demos are also *clean*. When you download a demo from a major site such as www.softseek.com, you know you're not getting a virus-ridden piece of junk; you're getting a clean, working version of the application or game or what-have-you. Can you feel as safe if you were to bypass the cracking process and just get the appz version? From "Jimmyz Anal Whore & Appz" homepage? I think not.

But why in hell do the big boys like Norton and our old friend M$ engage in the practice of distributing demos in the first place? Are they masochists? Sort of. They play the odds. If they get burned one time out of 500 then they come out on top. If they started getting burned say one time out of 50 . . . well, that would be a whole new kettle of application source code, now, wouldn't it? But most people are fine, upstanding citizens who would never steal a thing in their lives . . . even if it were staring them right in the face. So the big boys get richer and you get poorer. Further, Norton likes the *convenience* of distributing fully functioning software packages like Norton Utilities 98. Norton wants to get richer and richer. It does so by cornering the market. It will distribute demos and hook you in with the convenience of *remote registering*. You simply call their 1-800 number, burp out your Visa account number, and $70 later you get the registration code. That way, you see, Norton doesn't have you leaving the comfort of your little digital hidy-hole to get at your wallet. The fuckers.

But they didn't count on me. Me and my fucking crack. The only thing between you and the full version of the program is the registration code. So we need a *cracker program* (or "prog-gie," if you like to sound like an AOLer; it sounds like something a 3-year-old says, so I stay away from using it). You get crackers from the local h/p/v/c/a sites (as in *The Ultimate Internet Terrorist*). You then marry the two (zipped crackz are fully documented as shown elsewhere, don't worry) and voila! No shelling out $80 for software for you!

Hackers *love* this method. It works. It's easy. *Appz* are illegally duplicated applications (such as Office 97) which are complete and ready for you to install on your PC. They are very rare and time-consuming to find. Crackz, however, are everywhere; I defy you to type in "crackz" in a search engine of your choosing and not come up with something. See? I told you. Also, so you won't freak out when you see it in the wild, the nomenclature "crack house" is becoming quite popular. You will see sites such as: "Jimmyz Crack House" and/or "Don't be a Dick, Get Your Crack From Lil' Dickyz Warez, Crackz and Anal Site." It's just a play on words; such sites usually have nothing to do with drugs of any sort. Demos, likewise, are stupid-silly easy to get . . . direct from the manufacturer's FTP site!

The "crack" method of software theft is very prevalent. It's easy not to get caught. Think about it: you're bringing two *legal* things into your home, are you not? A demo program (provided by the manufacturer itself) and a "crack," which is a small, executable code module (no more than 20K). Then you're (not so legally) combining the two dear things in the privacy of your own home. What more could you possibly ask? Ahhhh . . . there's nothing like the feeling of seeing that "Thank you for your purchase!" screen pop up after a successful crack is run. You'll get to like that in a hurry. But be warned, you may never leave your Navigator browser as you find yourself looking for more and more crack!

GERMAN CRACKING FORCE / PC -ÄÄÄÜ

ÉÍÍÍÍÍÍÍÍÍÍÍÍÍÍÍÍÍÍÍÍÍÍÍÍÍÍÄ⁻ laxity / 08-98 ®ÄÍÍÍÍÍÍÍÍÍÍÍÍÍÍÍÍÍÍÍÍÍÍÍÍÍÍÍ»
° Date [22.08.98]   Cracked by [SONIC 98] °
° Titel [Norton AntiVirus v5.0 Win95/98 (Trial)   ] °
° I-Net [ftp://ftp.symantec.com/misc/americas/sabu/nav5/nav95tr.exe   ] °
° I-Net [ftp://ftp1.symantec.com/misc/americas/sabu/nav5/nav95tr.exe   ] °
° I-Net [ftp://ftp2.symantec.com/misc/americas/sabu/nav5/nav95tr.exe   ] °
ÍÍÍ◊
°   [ ] GAME [x] APPZ [ ] OTHER   °
°   [ ] REG NUMBA [x] CRACK [ ] KEY FILE [ ] KEY GENERATOR
° [   ] °
° [This crack removes the 30 days evaluation limit   ] °
° [   ] °
° [- Copy the NAV5_9x.COM to Symantec shared directory   ] °
° [(\Program Files\Common Files\Symantec Shared\ )   ] °
° [- Run the NAV5_9x.COM   ] °
° [   ] °
° [Have a nice day !   ] °

ÛÛ³ÉÍÍÍÍÍÍÍÍÍÍÍÍÍÍÍÍÍÍÍÍÍÍÍÍÄ⁻ Membaz: ®ÄÍÍÍÍÍÍÍÍÍÍÍÍÍÍÍÍÍÍÍÍÍÍÍÍ» ³ÛÛ
ÛÛ³⁰ Animalo   ³cracker, founder   ³Ü laxity_hq@gmx.net   ⁰³ÛÛ
ÛÛ³⁰ SONIC 98   ³cracker, iNET admin   ³Ü laxity_s98@gmx.net ⁰³ÛÛ
ÛÛ³⁰ pCsK8R   ³cracker   ³Ü laxity_pc@gmx.net   ⁰³ÛÛ
ÛÛ³⁰ Yaan!   ³cracker   ³Ü laxity_yaan@hotmail.com ⁰³ÛÛ
ÛÛ³⁰ JoGy   ³cracker   ³Ü jogy_laxity@hotmail.com ⁰³ÛÛ
ÛÛ³⁰ The Brain   ³cracker   ³Ü the.brain.@gmx.net   ⁰³ÛÛ
ÛÛ³⁰ xCrk   ³cracker   ³Ü xcrk@bigfoot.com   ⁰³ÛÛ
ÛÛ³⁰ vTeC   ³cracker   ³Ü @   ⁰³ÛÛ
ÛÛ³⁰ Swoop   ³cracker   ³Ü @   ⁰³ÛÛ
ÛÛ³⁰ Smakkker   ³cracker   ³Ü @   ⁰³ÛÛ
ÛÛ³⁰ Twister   ³cracker   ³Ü @   ⁰³ÛÛ
ÛÛ³⁰ Cygn   ³cracker   ³Ü @   ⁰³ÛÛ
ÛÛ³⁰ The Capitalist³cracker   ³Ü @   ⁰³ÛÛ

Figure 8. An actual ".nfo" [information] file from a crack program. Note the para-military stylized layout, roster, and ranking insignia (somewhat disguised).

But you're not a rocket scientist, now are you? No. You're just somebody who likes crack. You need *documentation* to use the crack. See Figure 8. This is an actual screen from such a document. You will always find these in the zipped crackz that you download from a hacker's site ("toggleMOUSEcrack.zip"). In the zip, you will see something to the effect of "c4a.nfo". That's shorthand for an INFORMATION file. You may click on it and start it as a Notepad file (the computer will prompt you to open it as something since .nfo is not a recognized file type). Opening a .nfo file will not harm you or your computer in any way. It's just a text file. The .nfo, as the example shows, will guide you from there. In short, you usually need to install the demo, NOT RUN IT (or exit out of the program if it runs automatically after you set it up), and unzip the crack.exe into the appropriate directory. Now it's just a matter of clicking on the "crack.exe" and letting the world fall into your devilish hands.

A successful crack is usually announced by a DOS window (the window that the crack.exe is running in) exclaiming "File successfully cracked!" or something similar. A "Finished" statement in the DOS header gives you the OK to exit out of DOS.

There are some subtle points to crackz that I need to clue you in to. First, sometimes the demo and the crack will be out of synch. What the hell does that mean? Well, demos get released in *versions*. You'll see things like "Norton Utilities V3.09". That "V" stands for version. The crack has to match the demo or you're screwed. A lot of the time you'll notice that the demo outruns the crack. In other words, you can download the demo V3.09, but the cracks are only up to V3.05. Oh Jesus! What to do? Get the demo. And wait. Wait for some kind hacker son-of-a-bitch to crack it. Then you're in business.

There's another method, however, and it's so insidious that I'm loathe to share it with you. Oh, what the hell–just go to the manufacturer's FTP site (remember our friend ftp://ftp.mcafee.com). You can do this on the Web with your browser. You don't need to drag out CuteFTP for this bullshit job. The FTP site will have (usually) *outmoded* versions that you may download to your heart's content. These are clearly marked in folders that look just like Windows Explorer. Common ones are "oldfiles" or "archive." So now you can get that V3.05 after all. You lucky son of a bitch!

Second (and I really shouldn't have to say this), people tend to get a little sloppy when it comes to security in this "field." You've all heard the urban legend (maybe it's true, but I don't give a rat's ass) about the coke head who gets robbed and loses his stash. He calls the cops and reports the stash as a stolen item. The cops sniff around (so to speak) and wind up arresting him on a variety of charges, not the least of which is paraphernalia and modified firearms possession. Well, kids, the same goddamn thing can happen to you with cracked software if you start to get complacent. Case in point–if you have Norton Anti-Virus cracked, for God's sake don't use "Live Update" to replenish the virus data; download the definition files from the FTP site yourself when your originals go stale. I don't know why, but some people think it's perfectly safe to act as though the stuff they have really is clean . . . as if the whole world will follow along with their own delusions. Just remember that some assholes think it's a-okay to sniff paint until their brains are leaking out their ears, too.

Understand that the above does not apply to *upgrading* cracked software. I know this cat who has MS Office Pro 97 floating around on CD, which he freely loans out. What good is 97? This is 99. Hell, you're missing the point. Once you have 97 Pro installed you can buy future upgrades from Worst Buy for $200 or so. (Incidentally, this same guy discovered a *backdoor* for all M$ products. The CD key is 1112-111111. For everything M$ puts out. Everything. Think about that for a second, will you? It's a delicious thing to ponder . . .)

Finally, understand that the term *patch* (see Dick's story below) and *crack* are so similar as to be indistinguishable. The only difference I've been able to discern is that patches are usually married to *gamez*, while crackz are usually used on *appz*. You'll hear hackers in chat rooms talk about "getting the fucking patch for MK5" or "cracking the hell out of Norton AV 6," for example. It boils down to the same thing in the final analysis.

That's the story in a nutshell. Unless you're a frigging retard or just flat-out don't give a shit, you'll find a thing or two out there without much trouble.

DICK'S ADVENTURES IN CRACKLAND

Let's talk about a guy named Dick. Dick is a computer buff, like you. He's not a genius (like Bill Gates) nor is he a fuckup (like AOLers). He's just an average surfer of yea olde WWW. One day Dick decided he'd like Addiction Pinball. He went to Worst Buy and found it cost $45. Dick didn't like that. He went away from the store empty handed and slightly depressed. He related this story in a chat room later that night. Someone in the room clued Dick into the topic of crackz. Dick liked what he heard. Dick was happy; he was a happy Dick.

Thus began Dick's adventures in Crackland. Dick was a pretty fast learner and downloaded the demo of Addiction from the Team 17 FTP site. It took a long time, but that was OK; Dick found it easy to wait for something he could brag about for days and that would give him the satisfaction of swearing off Worst Buy for good. Dick then searched in HotBot for the Addiction crack. He didn't find it, but he found something called a *patch* for Addiction. Dick got the patch. He unzipped it and was pleased to find there was ample documentation that explained how the patch could be applied. Dick was really starting to fly. He installed the demo of Addiction and then ran the patch against the executable (pinball.exe). The patch did some pretty funky things to the main executable. When Dick ran the pinball program, he expected that it would start right up and he could then play until falling into a coma later that evening.

But that didn't happen. The program simply came back with a very rude "Insert CD." Dick was a little miffed. Actually Dick was pretty fucking mad. He got on the horn to his hacker buddies. His hacker buddies told him he needed a CD crack. Dick didn't know what the fuck that was. His hacker buddies helped him find one through HotBot's search engine. Dick was grateful; he was a grateful Dick.

Dick unzipped the CD crack but only found a document inside. Curious, he read it in Notepad. It contained instructions to modify the pinball.exe program with a hex editor. So Dick needed to find a hex editor. He went to simtel.net and got a shareware version for Windows 95. He unzipped it and installed it. He ran it and opened pinball.exe. Dick then made the changes (in hex) that the CD crack document told him to do. It was a one-line change that even Dick could manage . . . even though he didn't know what "hex" was besides a curse a witch was supposed to put on people.

The hex editor refused to make the change. Dick's head started to hurt. Dick felt like punching someone. Dick was in a bad way. Now Dick had to find *another* hex editor–one that didn't require registration to edit files. You see, Dick had the poor fortune of finding a hex editor that demanded its author be paid before it would put out. Not good. Dick got another editor. This time it worked. Dick saved the change to the executable and ran the program (Addiction Pinball). Dick was able to play the game from dawn till dusk for the rest of his life. Dick was happy. Dick was enlightened. Dick was never the same. From then on he was able to crack just about anything. In fact it got to be sort of an addiction itself. Dick never had another piece of registered software on his PC again. He was a smart Dick.

The story of Dick is true. However, you should not infer it to imply the author or any associates of the author. The moral? I don't think there is one. I really don't.

APPZ AND GAMEZ

Appz, as I said, are full versions of registered software. You would download and install one of these as usual (as if you had paid for it, ahem). You can search for appz as usual, just don't expect miracles to occur at your feet. The safety issue with appz and/or crackz is a tough cookie to chew through, if you know what I mean. The only one way to find out is to scan such proggies with a virus scanner. Now that I think of it, you *could* buy a scanner straight from a store to "prime" your system . . . or you *could* take a chance and install a crack (demo virus shields are everywhere–get yours today from ftp://ftp.mcafee.com). That's a big chance, though; be careful!

Gamez are registered versions of current commercially available games. Gamez are similar to appz; both are pirated copies of someone's work. They're categorized differently so you know not to look for "Office Pro 2000" under "Gamez." Crackz, Appz, and Gamez all fall under the general term "Warez," since all are highly illegal.

THE DARKSIDE

Who would possibly have the audacity to operate and stock sites bubbling with illegal shit as far as the eye may see? The usual motley crew of bad-boy hackers, of course! They have neat little WWW sites with *framed menus* lettered in Gothic script: "Hackz, Appz, Gamez, XXX." The X-rated material just goes with the territory; these are high school and college kids for the most part and have the usual appetites of men that age. Some of these sites are clearly for real, some are in a gray area, and some are run by the feds and/or Micro$oft to catch YOU. I once found a site that was titled "The Micro$oft Phraud Page–if you came here looking for warez you are one lousy sucker!" and then went

Appz	Description / Sent in by ...	Size (KB)	Works?
1 Cool Button Tool	Little graphics tool used to make buttonz	589	Yes
3D Font FX	Make kewl new fonts and stuff	6020	Yes
3D Studio Max	A "PHAT" 3D rendering progie	5607	Yes
Adaptec Direct	CD-burning software!	3790	???
Adobe Acrobat	Read PDF formatted files	???	???

Figure 9. What you might see in a "warez" site. Note the file size is given to help you determine download times. The site gives some indication of the status of the product, as well ("Works?").

on to say that the site was even then being monitored, all connections were logged, and the police were on the way. What the hell was it? A hacker's twisted idea of a prank? The FBI's version of an electronic Venus fly-trap? I don't know, but I left rather quickly, just the same. Word to the wise: such a site may just serve to scare off the timid and may actually be a true warez site . . . but then again, with all those head games would you really trust such files on your computer?

A site like that may really (as in REALLY) log all incoming IP addresses. I hope you're using a proxy server. If so, then you have nothing to worry about. Actually, your odds of not getting any trouble from such a site are very, very good . . . but they'll still know who you are. And they'll come knocking if they have enough on you.

"Honest" warez sites, I've found, usually don't play games, don't have "TOP 55 Hacker Sites" banners (which open new browser windows like flowers on your screen), and don't issue petty threats. They just give you what you want right there and then. If the site requests you to follow them some place else, teases you about being the FBI or agents of M$, or demands that you waste time filling out your e-mail address, etc., for a "password," my God, run for your life! Odds are that *at least* you will be given bogus links designed to irritate you. Worse, the "downloads" will be filled with virii or, worse, *logic bombs* (see last chapter of this book) designed to torpedo your system straight to the farthest depths of Shoal. At worst you will receive a rather nasty call from the evil minions of Bill Gates . . .

An easy way of detecting fraudulent fraud sites (what a world, eh?) is to simply *roll* your mouse over the *underlined hot links*. This will show you where that particular file is coming from (where it's being linked from, in other words). Why is this important? If the link shows that the file is coming from "shareware.com" you know that the file is useless. In other words it's *uncracked shareware*; just the raw demo version. Why would someone bother posting such a waste of time? To look like a tough guy. To look "bad." As in: "Look at me: I'm so bad I've got WAREZ on my homepage at earthlink.net." The trouble is, the kid in question doesn't have the balls to post a real warez link, so he just posts a fake. Most people are fooled; they don't check the source file before downloading. You should see people's faces when I first clue them into the whole world of warez and crackz: they walk around like they've just discovered the secrets to the universe for a week or so. They then download anything from warez sites. And they get screwed. And then they bitch at me, as if I'm the source of all this confusion. Don't be like them; be a smart shopper.

Personally, while doing research for this book, I found that using an *FTP search engine* such as "Filez.com" churned out much better results in the warez department than Web links could ever do. But always examine the *full path* of such a match, such as:

ftp://ftp.test.warez.au/incoming//ibm/**win/95**/msoffice/word7/crackz/
ftp://ftp.test.warez.au/incoming/ibm/**linux**/msoffice/word7/crackz/

The bold is added to make a point. If a criminal were looking to steal MS WORD 7 for Windows 95, which would he/she choose? That extra bit of attention narrows down search times considerably. Using tremendously powerful search engines such as "The Dogpile" and selecting to search "FTP THEN STOP" speeds up search times dramatically (it will not return the usually bogus WWW matches, in other words).

Remember, I never told you any of this . . . and I wish to hell and back I had one of those *Men in Black* gizmos to use when I open my big mouth too far.

THE FUNNIEST THING IN THE WORLD

Just as an ending thought, remember how we looked at the ways cybercriminals justify their actions involving MP3s? Believe it or not, "crack sites" justify their actions as well. How? This will absolutely kill you, so I hope you haven't eaten recently. They say (and I'm not making this up; I'm just not that smart) they provide crackz for legitimate owners of software that have–over the years–lost their serial number or CD master disk. CD? What's that have to do with anything? CDs are usually how these programs are purchased and, sometimes, are required every time you run the program. Thus, if you had that particular application (computer program) over several years and lost the CD you could not use the program again.

Unless it were to be . . . cracked.

Get it? They actually have the balls to say they're providing a service to the end-user community. And with that I will leave you to throw up (hopefully not all over this book).

CHAPTER THREE

XXX FILES

The Adults-Only Internet

IT STARTS THE SECOND YOU get online. You start seeing porno banners in 3D with full-motion, sound . . . and explicit scenes beyond comprehension of mere mortals.

Do you click on them? Of course you do. I'll spare you the grisly details of what lies in store for you (as if you don't already know), but you're just one of untold thousands that click on them everyday . . . hell, every *second*. Does that sound outrageous? It isn't; last year the growth of pay-only sex sites went up 900 percent. *In one year*. The money is rated in the *billions*. We'll explore this side of the 'net in some lurid detail in this section. We'll talk about the legality of this side of things, what stupid people do . . . and, most importantly, what *smart* people do.

HARDCORE

Yes, you can find any explicit sexual act on today's 'net. Don't ask me why on earth humans invest countless hours bringing something as low-tech as sexual relations to every possible new bit of technology that comes along. I couldn't tell you. It started with still pictures, quickly made it over to early motion pictures, was the first thing you could buy for an early Beta VCR and then, of course, the Internet. The Internet (WWW and FTP sites) became, overnight, the largest repository of every imaginable human congress. This includes bestiality, child porn, S&M, and every thing else under the sun. Faked celebrity nude shots are currently the "in thing," and Alyssa Milano is suing as I speak. Suing whom? The Internet?

Is this stuff even legal? Why that's a knot! Legal *where*? On the Internet? And just where *is* the Internet, by the way? On the moon? In Bill Gates' garage? "On a computer someplace?" It's everywhere. It's nowhere. Ask Alyssa Milano.

It's immaterial, something not of this world. You can't hold it in your hand, and you couldn't possibly mail a letter to it. Try it sometime:

> INTERNET
> PO BOX 1307
> BOULDER, CO 80306 c/o Alyssa Milano

Does that make sense? Of course not. But we *can* affect it somehow. We can add to it. We can take away from it. But it's always there. Are you as confused about the question of legality on the Internet as when you started reading this section? Are you? Good. You should be, since it is a question with no possible answer. My advice: you want to see something that gets you off, go look for it; it'll be there. You are offended by the mention of the word "intercourse"? Then don't go lookin' for it because it's not looking for you. I suppose I could summarize my view of legal issues and the 'net simply by making the metaphor: Don't mess with Texas . . . and Texas won't mess with you.

GETTING CONNECTED

Odds are you will want to view some of the aforementioned material. What's the best way? Well, we'll get to that in a tik, but right now let's look at the wrong way . . . which is signing up for these services with your credit card.

Don't do it! Besides all the nasty info you should already know from reading my first book, *The Ultimate Internet Terrorist*, you should know some more things that pertain especially to the darkest of Darksides . . .

In the first place, you'll be paying for recycled trash pictures from Usenet. These are "newsgroups" accessible via Dejanews.com and are open to the public. Common-sense sites are alt.binaries.erotica.facial.cum and alt.pictures.suffocation.celebs. Your basic porno on the 'net. Don't be ashamed; heck, we've all wanked off to picture or two like that in our past. But far from the quality one may expect from modern, moderately budgeted porno flicks you rent in the curtained-off area of the video store where you live, these are crummy, hard-to-make-out shots taken in someone's basement or backyard. If you want to see these pictures, just HotBot "usenet archives adult hardcore" which will return plenty of porno for free. Also try "newshog adult archives." Same deal.

The formula your typical pay-only site uses is as follows (this *will* be on the final):

1) Copy tons of useless, junk .jpg pictures from Usenet.
2) Steal whatever else is available from legit sources (such as still shots from copyrighted porno films).
3) Use MicroSucks FrontPage 4.19 to draw a pretty, colored, dancing-lights Web page.
4) Go to geocities.com and get some free space, posting a page and paying a small amount for extra space to keep their "product."
5) Spam everyone to death (using techniques discussed in "Information Security" elsewhere in this book) with advertisements for their "site."
6) Distribute banners on other sleazy, low-budget sites.
7) Laugh while collecting credit card numbers from dummies who click on their banners and respond to their spam-mail.

Jaded? Cynical? No: *realistic*.

A BETTER WAY

Smart people know better than to pay out cold cash to slick sites that advertise with banners on the Web. Smart people know these assholes are just taking your money and smiling. Smart people know about two things: backdoors and password sites.

PASSWORDS, PASSWORDS EVERYWHERE . . .

Password sites? Excuse me? Well, these are Web pages provided at no cost (they have heavy advertisers from cyber casinos, virtual pimps, and other take-your-money crap services) by various hacking groups (common) or loners (rare). They usually have "warez," "mp3z," and "hacking, cracking, virus, and anarchy" (remember *The Ultimate Internet Terrorist?*) sections, as well as "passwords" or "XXX," which is the focus of this chapter. The "passwords" section is simply an HTML file consisting of hundreds of hot-links that will provide you with "other means" of ingress into pay-only adult Web sites. In other words, they are virtual trading posts for stolen passwords just begging to be used . . .

Yes, there are actually hundreds of these sites, most of which are in plain view. Just HotBot "password sites" or "xxx megapass" or go into Dejanews.com and search for "password sites & XXX." Works every time. What do you find in a place like "megapass"? A huge, totally FREE Web page with sections such as "Today's Verified Links," "Old Links I," Old Links II," etc. When you explore further, you will find a page like Figure 10.

Clicking on a hot-link will open that service instantly. Notice that the passwords themselves are also linked, but you *may* have to type it in again if a dialog box should open. Just right-click the hot-link (remember my admonishments in *Ultimate Internet Terrorist* to always right-click while on-line?) and use "Open in New Browser." Now cycle back and forth (ALT+TAB) between browser windows to get the password and login ID correct. When I say "passwords are linked," I mean something like this:

http://fuck:you@www.cumfacials.com/archives/blowjobs/dir

The colon separates the *login* and *password*. The two go through automatically, thus saving you the headache of remembering two words from three seconds ago.

NOTE: If a username/password has a "@" - you must manually login

SITE	USERNAME	PASSWORD	ADDED
Bwatch.com	firm	tits	14:33:38/3-Feb-99
205.152.12.213	test	tester	13:25:30/3-Feb-99
Celebrityx.com	allthefin	waydude	13:25:26/3-Feb-99
Karasxxx.com	detroit	lions	13:23:31/3-Feb-99
Babylon-x New	allthefin	waydude	13:23:27/3-Feb-99

Figure 10. A "password" site disseminating stolen/hacked accounts to XXX services on the Web. This risky stuff and probably worth a bust if you do it too much.

Are these "password sites" even legal? Not even remotely! If you're caught using these techniques they'll pull the switch on you without a trial. Believe it! This is so since you are: 1) engaging in willful fraud and 2) knowingly stealing a product or service via phone lines. Need I say more?

But when used with caution (i.e., proxy servers as described elsewhere in this book or a public Internet connection a la *The Ultimate Internet Terrorist*), these sites are bitchin'. And it'll be "bitchin'" when you get caught, too.

OUT THE BACKDOOR

Backdoors are even more fun. If you look at computers as more than just another appliance, you'll really get into this method. Check this out. A typical Web site could be:

http://www.cumfacials.com

If we were dummies off the street still using AOL, we would go to this *frontdoor*, give them our credit card number, and wave goodbye to several hundred dollars. All for junk pictures some simpleton jerk copped off every other adult site . . . and most of that can be traced back to Usenet's public archives.

Backdoors, on the other hand, allow us to break into the protected, "members-only" area of that site. How? With a degree in solid-state engineering? No, just common sense. Here's what I'm talking about:

http://www.cumfacials.com/pp/members/protected/pictures/archives/blowjobs/dir/

Talk about a mouthful! If you type that whole thing into Netscape and press ENTER you will have by-passed all security for that site in one roll of the dice. You'll go directly to the pictures archive, instead of taking the long road of first viewing their main page (http://www.cumfacials.com), signing up, clicking on "members-only," etc. Weeeee! In my ecstasy, I will now quote the great Zen Buddhist monk Homer Simpson by saying, "All this computer hacking is making me thirsty. Where's my TAB?"

Some keywords you may try are: members, archives, pictures, unlocked, images, blowjobs, anal, straight.

Now, being an impatient American reader, you will attempt this once and it will not work. Then you will e-mail/phone me complaining that my book "doesn't work." Oh, please, Mr. Jackass, stay on the line so I can find you and kill you.

Duh! Of course it won't work the first time out! You have to experiment, and you have to work at cracking out your own catch-codes. I'm just a simple guy here helping you so you're not as blind as you were before my book came along. That's it.

Give me a fucking break here, people!

But I have to get you started, so here goes. First change the http:// to a ftp:// and hit ENTER. So first it read: http://www and now it reads ftp://www. If successful, it will list the directory in "Windows File Manager"-like format.

CumFacials
parent directory
^____

GuestsMembers
etc. . . .

Now by clicking on "members" you will find a subdirectory:

Members
parent directory
^____

Archive 1
Archive 2
Archive 3
etc. . . .

Clicking on these will reveal more and more "layers" of the site. You may also try gopher:// in place of ftp:// (although it will probably not work as well).

A backdoor is not the same thing as using a password (which makes a hell of a lot of sense since we don't type in a password anywhere along the yellow brick road) and, as such, avoids a lot of the legal hassles. I recommend backdoors highly. What this comes down to is exploiting a loophole, straight and simple. We may wrangle back and forth a little about the ethics of who's right and who's wrong in this, but the fact remains, if it's so damn important, they should lock it up. You can make analogies until the cows come home: locking the door but leaving a window open in your home, dropping a wallet on a sidewalk, leaving the keys in your unlocked car, etc.

Hey, you figure it out. If you need me I'll be cracking out sites . . .

INFORMATION SUPER SECURITY
Staying Safe in an Unsafe World

YOU ARE A SITTING DUCK RIGHT NOW, and you don't even know it. You poor bastard. How? Count the ways: someone could be going through your hard-drive contents while you're away. Hackers of all manners (and crooked system operators) can and are watching your IP (Internet protocol) address at every turn, seeing where you go and how you got there. Spam junk mailers are clogging your e-mail account with gobs of sexually suggestive e-mail and other nonsense that takes *your* time to sift through.

Wouldn't you like to stop them?

I'll bet you would, so I'll show you how to stop *all* these sons-a-bitches, and many more . . .

AGGRESSIVE E-MAIL

I hate junk mail. And junk phone calls. Just as an aside, that's why I recently bought a modem, which acts as a total communications center: it screens my calls, doesn't ring until I say it may, has Caller ID built in, and so much more that I tittered like an insane schoolgirl while I installed the thing. You may purchase one of these modems yourself for around $80 and install it easily. But don't ever pay for someone to install a modem; it's like paying for someone to check your tire's air pressure: if you have the cognitive ability above a gila monster, you can do it yourself. I recommend 3COM, but any speaker-phone/message center rated at 56K and V.90 will do the trick.

But then there's e-mail. Oh my God, e-mail! The age of e-junk mail has arrived, and by the time you read this you will be awash in it, I am positive. So let's stop it. In my last book (read it, baby, read it!) I mentioned the process of using *filters* to screen out your e-mail, but here I want to REALLY take you through the run of things. That way you can do it yourself. I will use a very generic format to save time and space; you'll just have to see what works for your particular application. I can't hold your hand forever, sweety.

In order to use a filter effectively, you must first identify who's doing it to you. The best way (and I speak from very practical application of this method) is to click on "more details," which will produce a screen like the one in Figure 11. This allows you to see (as illustrated) the origin of the junk mail. It is an IP address, as shown, and can be converted using a <u>Name Server</u> (NS) gateway to American English. This will show you who's doing it. A Name Server gateway may be found, not too unsurprisingly, by typing in the words "name server gateway" in HotBot and letting nature take its course. After you find the gateway, type in the IP and hit "submit." This will return the English version of the IP. For example, 203.123.12.1 run through the NS might equal startrek.junk-mail.com

You may type in the offending origin IP (203 . . .) or converted form (startrek . . .) in Netscape. This *may* take you to the site directly but will more than likely result in a *dialog box* (see elsewhere) popping up and asking for a password before you may proceed. This is simply a firewall and is designed to protect the people spamming you with junk mail. They're cowards, you see.

No matter. Just type in the IP of the assholes in your filter window as shown. Batta-bing-batta-bang! No more junk mail.

While you're there, create another filter (as shown below) to delete automatically any e-mail with such catch phrases as

Received: from smtp.snet.net [204.60.33.21] by mx03 via mtad (2.6)
  with ESMTP id mx03-cLwXLh0083; Wed, 23 Dec 1998 23:11:33 GMT

Received: from pop.snet.net (pop.snet.net [204.60.33.22])
  by smtp.snet.net (8.9.1a/8.9.1/SNET-bmx-1.3/D-1.6/O-1.3) with ESMTP id SAA00279
  for <rmerkle@usa.net>; Wed, 23 Dec 1998 18:11:31 -0500 (EST)

Received: from sjh (brpt-sh2-port137.snet.net [204.60.23.137])
  by pop.snet.net (8.9.1a/8.9.1/SNET-pop-1.3/D-1.5/O-1.3) with ESMTP id SAA09423
  for <rmerkle@usa.net>; Wed, 23 Dec 1998 18:11:30 -0500 (EST)

Message-Id: <199812232311.SAA09423@pop.snet.net>
From: "Sjh" <sjh@snet.net>
To: <rmerkle@usa.net>
Subject: book
Date: Wed, 23 Dec 1998 17:58:20 -0500

Figure 11. The important item here is "Received: from: smtp.snet.net [204.60.33.21]" at the top (below the banner) which shows WHO this ungodly son of a bitch really is. You can then type that IP into your browser and hit the magical enter key. Lazarus, come forth!

"free" or "xxx" or "x" or "adult" in the *subject window*. This is very effective. Also, check the box that requests your e-mail address be taken off *known junk-mailers'* lists. You must do this; it is vital. It is the first thing you need to do *now*; I will wait.

Sometimes the bastards are pretty clever, though. From time to time, you'll get an e-mail (almost always advertising a sex site) which will, helpfully, say "If you wish to stop receiving these e-mails, please reply with 'Remove' in the subject window." MY GOD, WHATEVER YOU DO, DON'T FOLLOW THEIR ADVICE! If I could reach out from this page and grab you by the throat until you got it, I would. Don't do it!

You see, they're playing the oldest gambit in the world: finding a needle in a haystack. Paradoxically, you'll notice a message that has such "advice" for you really isn't addressed to you. It's addressed to "you@host.com" or "person@place.com" or maybe just "YOU" in the "To:" field. The real address is an "address book"-style list of e-mail addys . . . with you in there

59

PERSONAL OPTIONS AND FEATURES

Settings:
>   Account options related to e-mail handling, junk mail blocking, and account status.

Your Profile:
>   Information about you that helps us provide a better, more relevant service.

Password:
>   This is where you change your log-in password. Practice good security by changing this on a regular basis.

Signatures:
>   Set up personal signatures that can be attached to outgoing mail. You can have different signatures for personal mail, business

Figure 12. Note the "Settings" option is the one we want to make our very own filter.

YOUR CURRENT MAIL FILTERS

When the Sender's Address Contains "153.36.",
>   Delete   Active

When the Sender's Address Contains "207.68.143.178",
>   Delete   Active

When the Sender's Address Contains "wolfram.com",
>   Delete   Active

When the Subject Contains "free x",
>   Delete   Active

Figure 13. And this is what we end up with, a successful filter or two. Note the "free x" filter which prevents porn from offending my virgin eyes. The action on all filters is to automatically *delete* incoming mail.

somewhere. God knows where. And by responding to it you will stand out. Big-time. They'll tag you as a "sucker" and put you on the sucker list. The one they trade with all the other junk-mailers. Then . . . oh, and then! You'll receive mail from the furthermost reaches of the cosmos, from places not of this world. Use my method above: get into the "details" of how the message got to you. Block out the origin IP. Problem solved.

Now, with some *legitimate* businesses, cyber or real, it is a wise policy to request that they cease sending e-mail. Such places include electronics stores (either virtual or physical) where you may have made a purchase and then included your e-mail for verification purposes. Sometimes such places will send you a reminder to upgrade your product (whatever it may be) every so often, warranty information, etc. That's not a problem. But then some may get a little too friendly with you. That's when a simple "stop it or else I'm coming for you" letter works magic. I've been forced once or twice to fire off such e-mails to legitimate companies I knowingly gave my addy to, and it worked. It's obvious you know who they are in this case, so they will always stop. But sometimes wires get crossed and the company may still send junk warranty information to your addy, trade your addy to other companies, etc. If this happens never do business with such a company in the future and warn your fellow humans by posting the story of your dilemma on Usenet (Dejanews.com is great for this). Block the origin IP using a filter as shown above.

This whole process is referred to in the hacking community (both legitimate as in programmer and system design "hackers" and illegitimate as in Darkside "hackers") as *anti-spam*. Spam, as detailed in my previous book, is simply the sending of many needless, wasteful messages. Like the food name, this is pretty nasty stuff (although fried and dressed with ham glaze it's decent). Ahem. Spam may refer to your telephone as well, as the introduction to this section alluded to. Salespeople "spam" me all the time over the phone (well, they still try their hardest I should say). At its worst, spam degenerates rapidly into *e-mail bombing*, as it destroys your e-mail account. At the level we're talking about, it's just called cyber junk mail. It won't clog your account like molasses in a carburetor but, man, it sure is a pain in the arse to deal with . . . as I'm sure I don't need to remind you, right?

As for the future of e-mail security and counterintel ops, consider, if you will, the following: to exacerbate the already tangled mess of identities, e-mail, and never knowing who the hell is on the other end of the computer, we now have WWW services that will sell you a custom e-mail address. Big deal, right? Wrong: for a small price I can get jim@lawyer.com or robert@uclamedschool.com and just about anything else. Now I can get on a newsgroup and start charging for legal and or/ medical advice. Funnny. Real funny. Try www.mail.com if you want to impress your friends that you are now jamessw@cia.com. Opportunities in terms of information security monkey-wrenching are endless using this method. Just think of all the trouble I could cause by having an e-mail addy like billclinton@whitehouse.gov or monical@whitehouse.gov, but remember before you get too carried away that your IP will always show through as we saw in the filter screen shots above.

ELECTRONIC SAFES

Is someone spying on you? Prying into your hard-drive contents, sizing you up, wondering what in the hell you're up to with all those MP3 files and porno JPEG.? Can't happen? Okay how about this, hot-shot: you take your POS 9000 in after a year for a memory upgrade and modem install. Pretty routine. But technicians are an unsavory lot; they are usually social misfits, shunned by the opposite sex and unable to achieve an erection without prying in to someone else's personal effects. They snoop. And the things they see in people's computers! My lord, the things they see! Could you imagine, just imagine, mind you, what someone would see in *my* computer? I'd be locked up for life!

You're probably not as degenerate as I am (it just isn't possible), but you should still have some type of safe-deposit box for your files. In this section we'll explore the many ways of doing this. Remember, the term "e-safe" will refer to a concept, not to a particular product, name-brand, or software application. We'll look at three major methods.

The first is store-bought or downloaded applications such as "SureStore." This is pretty good . . . but not great. Yes, you get everything in a package; it has a pretty GUI (graphical user interface), which looks like a bank vault and works . . . it just isn't "hackerish." These work simply by dragging and dropping a file (or entire directory) onto the "bank-vault" icon that is created on your desktop when the application is installed. These may be downloaded off the WWW as shareware or bought shrink-wrapped in a store (not recommended; see my previous book for the DOs and DON'Ts of downloading and buying off-the-shelf software). They use a simple-simon encryption scheme that is blown away like a Dremel tool going through a Masterlock by the CIA, FBI, or NSA. I recommend this method for the average computer user but not for someone who likes his MP3s hot and his JPEGs even hotter. Ahem.

The second way we may keep nosy @ssholes out of our stuff is called *file encryption*. Underground programs distributed on hacker sites on the WWW may generate encryption. These are referred to as "hackware" programs that are provided at no charge. As *The Ultimate Internet Terrorist* stated, the key to finding such sites is to type in "h/p/v/c/a" under HotBot.

Individual files are encrypted, sometimes with a command-line under DOS such as:

```
c:>zapper sex.jpg
```

"Zapper" is the executable program that makes the music, such as "zapper.exe" somewhere on your hard drive, and sex.jpg is the file you want hidden.

You may also drag and drop the file onto the icon of the executable encryption generator, much like the "bank vault"-style kidware program above.

This method will stop ANYONE without a security clearance and the knowledge to use main-frame de-encryption methods. This means that unless you are Ted Kaczynski, me, or Bill Gates, you're safe. And, brother, you can take that to the bank!

A happy medium between methods one and two would be the program called "Encrypt It!" Hackers swear by it, but it's from Canada, and–get this, folks–you can't buy it outside their country! They say it has something to do with "export licensing," and if that isn't corporate slang for "the FBI can't break the cipher so the public can't have it," I don't know my head from a used condom. Encrypt It! is an extremely easy-to-use program that makes quick and fun use of a GUI under Windows 95/98 (a GUI is how the program looks to the user, like Netscape, etc.). It uses a password system, meaning you select which files (a la Windows Explorer) you wish to safeguard and the program scrambles them. Your password is the only thing that may unscramble them. Be careful; forget the password and you're in trouble! Are there backdoors at work here? Can the Canadian Solicitor General simply type in "masterkey" in place of your password and decrypt your top-secret files? Well, like I said, the Canadians can't even let you *download a trial version* of Encrypt It! so I doubt something like that can happen. Twocows.com has an old prototype copy they loan out to people in the know just to show it off. I can't say anything more; THEY are watching my every move . . .

The next method requires some creative thought and effort on your part. It's more of a fun exercise than anything else and will result in many a rainy afternoon spent experimenting with different methods. It's the *Poor Man's James Bond* method of electronic safe-deposit boxes. One such way I hit on in *The Ultimate Internet Terrorist* is to simply "zip" or compress your files. Use WinZip to accomplish this. To relative novices, a zipped file is quite baffling, but lots of people know about file compression, so don't trust this method too far. You may also–as a bonus to our loyal customers–compress (that is, "zip") entire directories at once. So, instead of dragging-and-dropping your JPEGs one at a time, just place all your bestiality pictures in one directory (don't call it "bestiality" though) and drop *that* directory into WinZip. Ha!

An improvement on this is to use another compression scheme than ".zip." Use ".lha" or ".arj". These will confuse the common Pkunzip or WinZip-using snoopster, thus rendering it useless. To use this method, you must procure the proper ".arj" compression utility. Use HotBot as usual (that should be like a reflex at this point) to find these.

Another way to escape and evade the snoopsters in your life is to *rename* your sensitive file/directories with dummy names: "sex.jpg" becomes "test.bin" or something equally innocous. WARNING: You *must* remember what you renamed your files. Without having it down somewhere in some form, you will never, in ten thousand lifetimes, be able to find it again. I am serious. On the street-level end of things, just renaming a *directory* itself can do the trick. For example, "XXX Files" becomes "spool" or "bin" and is then buried five layers deep. This will confound *some* of the vile snoops in your life . . . but hardly all. Simply using Windows Explorer and "Finding" all .jpg (images) files will sniff you out faster than a bloodhound. Better to *rename* your files so a .jpg or .doc search is pointless.

To clarify, when I say "five layers deep" I mean:

c:\images\xxx\cumshots\ a.jpg, b.jpg, c.jpg . . .

Becomes:

c:\win\system\spool\data\bin\ a.bin, b.bin, c.bin . . .

Your files would not be altered or compressed using this method.

SECRET COMMUNICATION

Private communication on the Internet is becoming quite difficult these days . . . and will become increasingly so over the following years. As you already know, if you haven't been living in a cave on Mars for the last decade or so, you can *not* trust e-mail for sensitive/embarrassing communications; it is routinely monitored by system administrators, the FBI, and God knows who else. This is not idle talk, folks, it is cold fact. Any mention of "key words" such as gun, attack, ammonia, President, bomb, or terrorist will get you noticed. Further talk will get a tap put on your e-mail account so fast Tim McVeigh will be asking for a roll of toilet paper and a box of matches from the next cell over before you know what went wrong.

What to do? Use an application called "Pretty Good Privacy" to encrypt your e-mail. This is an actual software program that you may download. Once you install and run this program, it will generate a "key" from which your message is encrypted. It all works like this: you have a telephone in your home, and you may use it to call someone else with a telephone. "PGP" allows you to call anyone with a phone (read: e-mail address), while the person on the other end is the only one who may "pick up" the ringing phone. When someone sends you a PGP-encrypted message, it's like answering your own phone . . . while no one else in the world may pick up your phone in your home.

PGP is perfect for those everyday clandestine communiqués over public phone lines, but what about the sender and receiver's identity? Will PGP protect you then? NO! Your sending IP (as discussed in detail above under the section concerning antispam techniques) will act as an e-beacon, pointing to your front door. Your partner on the other end? Ditto, in spades. Just think: your husband is even now busily rummaging through all your "sent" messages . . . which are saved PERMANENTLY by In-Box and Eudora Pro. Yep, I said permanently; I don't stutter, huxster. There's a little file inside every computer built today with Eudora installed called "trashcan.mbx," and that baby has every piece of mail you send, receive . . . and delete. Be sure to thank the makers of Eudora, right? Sheesh! More like shoot them in the streets like dogs.

But we have to deal with it. There are several methods. The first is to not use Eudora. We talked about that at length in *The*

Ultimate Internet Terrorist, but for those of you who don't know, you should be using a "webmail service" which is a free service on the WWW. Such services are Hotmail.com and Netaddress.com. You sign on for free and make up a phony name. No one will ever know it's you . . . unless they dig up the origin IP (see above).

But Kurt Saxon introduced me to a world of thought which is loads of fun to explore. To put it simply, there are folks who love to fantasize about, in Saxon's words, "functioning in an extreme totalitarian, Big Brother world." Well, Kurt would be proud if he could see this. Here's my super-duper, *Poor Man's James Bond* way of communicating in total secrecy. You need to procure a software application called "Anon Post." You use HotBot to find this on the WWW. If you had no trouble finding and installing an FTP client program, then this will be a snap. If you haven't mastered the WWW enough to do that, then you're probably wasting time by using a computer in the first place. Anon Post allows us to post–anonymously of course–to Usenet, which we talked about earlier in this book.

So what? Well, here's so what: you can, with minimal effort, *create* your own newsgroup. Use Anon Post or Dejanews.com to accomplish this. If using Dejanews.com, you will first need to login. This requires an e-mail address. Always offer a "webmail" address for this, *never* your Internet Service Provider's e-mail account you got when you signed up (such as "tommy@earth-link.net"). The group should be obscure without being notice-able. Names such as "rec.tomato growers of USA" would be a good choice. "alt.Freedom Bombers for Tim McVeigh" would be something to avoid. Now, using Anon Post, you may post two-way untraceable communiqués over Usenet. This is like the venerable electronic bulletin (message) board, or "BBS," of yore. You would post to your "homemade" alt.whatever group and wait for your lesbian lover to respond. No hassles. No incriminating evidence. No traces of you. Heh heh heh. Ain't the 'net grand?

BECOMING INVISIBLE

Now, I realize I'm a total computer and Dungeons & Dragons nerd, but I have to tell you: I *loved* the idea of an "invisibility spell" from the old D&D days.

You can become invisible on the World Wide Web.

Yep. I'll show you how to do it. It's something called a "proxy server." Proxy? Sounds like a prescription cough remedy doesn't it? Needless to say, it has nothing to do with the pharmaceutical industry. A "proxy" is something that may act on your behalf. Living the good life "by proxy" may mean being a live-in butler to an ultra-wealthy family. A "proxy" in the legal sense may mean someone to stand in on a court proceeding and who has your consent to state things in your place. A proxy does everything for your benefit . . . without *physically* being you. In this case, a proxy is another host computer or *server* that bounces a Web page off itself and into your computer. Look at Figure 14.

Notice how goddamn beautiful this system is? There's no way on Earth anybody at www.anywhere.com can figure out who you are. No way in hell.

No sweat, right? Wish you could have something like this yourself? Sure you do; there are dangers everywhere out there. But remember this only works for the WWW and not the Internet. There's a reason; a "proxy" server will cast that D&D spell of invisibility *while you're on the WWW* . . . not while using an FTP client! I can't stress that enough: if you start up CuteFTP while your proxy is doing its thing, man, you'll be naked as the proverbial jaybird the whole while. A proxy will protect a WWW browser (such as Netscape) only.

Now, I know you're probably dreading the technical discussion to come, sick and tired of the tech-talk and the buzz words and the acronyms that mean nothing to you . . . but setting up a proxy is easier than you think! It really is! Okay, you got me, I'm lying through my teeth: it's harder than hell. BUT for those who can bear with me, it *will* be worth it.

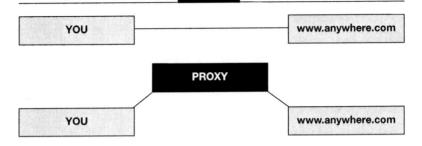

Figure 14. The concept of "indirect surfing."

A proxy:

1) Is FREE
2) Requires NO sign-up of ANY KIND
3) Has NO hourly-restrictions or site-style restrictions
4) Will NOT slow down your browser
5) Affords IMPENETRABLE security
6) Is 100-percent LEGAL and SAFE to use

Now what do you think? Think you can manage to hold your lunch down for a few minutes of your so God-awful precious time? Great. Thanks. Thanks a bunch. I'm only trying to save your life here, folks. To start, know this: Netscape *wants* you to use a proxy server. They really do! No BS; just get your arse in gear and start up Netscape Navigator Gold 3.x. Now click on "Options - Network - Proxies." SEE? I hate to gloat but: SEE? It's all ready for you. If you had the wherewithall, you could select: "manual proxy - VIEW" and be surfing to your invisible heart's content. SEE?

But you're not ready yet; you don't even know where to begin. So, to begin, go into Metacrawler.com and search for "proxy servers" and "hiding IP." That's the best (and only) way I know of to set you down the path of this strange, forgotten world (a world so strange and forgotten that the designers of

Netscape Navigator forgot to tell *you* about it). Am I right? Of course I am.

Now, what will come back for your trouble is a list of sites. Click on them, visit them, explore them. Sooner or later (it'll be sooner, trust me) a site will come forth offering you a chance to use their *proxy server*. That's when the fun begins. The site will go to great lengths, offering help at every conceivable step of the way, to show you how to fill in those funny "configure manual proxy" field boxes.

The downside to all this malarkey? You have to fill in the login and password *every single time* you open a browser session but NOT every time you change sites (surf the Web). It's a small price to pay, believe me. So, assuming we have configured our manual proxy and logged in successfully, what may we expect? You will surf normally and with no change in your usual connection speed. You will not go faster or slower by any amount. You will, however, see the proxy server address (URL) flash periodically in the gray status bar under the browser window, but that's to let you know it's alive and kicking. What will the people on the other end of this stick of dynamite see? Oh, this is real cute: just the IP of the proxy server, not yours in any fashion whatsoever! Weeee!!

One last thing: if someone plugs the IP (the proxy server's IP, that is) into a *Name Server* (NS) *Lookup gateway*, it will return as a possible "alias" IP. That means people will know you're running with something over you . . . like a mask. Remember, though, that using a proxy server is *not* illegal in the slightest; as we've seen, the manufacturer of Navigator saw fit to code proxy support right in there with all the rest of God's creative bounty. No one will screw with you (not that they could do anything about it anyway), but you should know that the hard-core cyber gunslingers out there will ask some odd questions if you attract their attention. They'll wonder who you "really" are, talk to you like one of their own kind, and genuinely be curious. Just ignore them and walk the other way. They can't do a thing to you. (If you'd like to know more about the ins and outs of this crowd of happy-go-lucky folks, then I refer you to *The Ultimate Internet Terrorist*).

That's invisibility in this day and age. For the price, this method is well worth it. Just remember that the proxy server operators can and do keep logs of who calls, how long, and where, so don't e-mail bomb threats to the president and you should be a-okay.

But the *real* pros have high-tech James Bond-style gadgets at their disposal. I want to introduce you to one of these in particular: the *firewall*, and it's exactly what you're thinking of. In this case, the "fire" is someone (or just a mindless computer server) outside of your PC trying to get in. They will attempt to steal your files and/or crash your system for good. Others may simply be nosey and attempt to penetrate you with a "finger" (see *The Ultimate Internet Terrorist*) to determine your identity. That's not good. Firewalls in years past were exclusively for the use of large corporate or government computer networks which, of course, had a lot to lose when it came to hackers off the street coming in and wreaking havoc. These companies would spend millions hiring elite programmers and security experts to set up their electronic firewalls.

They work like this: say there was an insurance salesman trying to sell some of his junk to a corporate big-wig. First the insurance guy would have to go through the general telephone receptionist, then the outer office assistant, then the big-wig's personal assistant, until he finally got through to the big-wig himself. That's firewall protection: you have to get through *something* to get at the target. That *something* should be resilient enough to withstand forceful attempts at entry before crashing (not impossible to beat, just very, very hard). Same deal with a network connection. *You* are the big-wig and the nosy site administrator is the insurance salesman. The receptionist is the firewall.

Now, thank God, more and more companies are coming out with *PC firewall applications*. Norton and ConSeal are two I recommend highly, although ConSeal has the superior track record for "unbeatable" security. Either of these affords your home computer the same protection usually reserved for large companies that are masked behind layers of electronic screening systems. Believe me, folks, nothing is finer at any price (especially if you get the crack).

A PC firewall will insulate you from numerous outside evils, such as hostile Java scripting (lines of code that will manipulate your computer via Internet like so much mindless plastic) and *cookies* (electronic markers created when you browse), which will track your every move on the Web. It will also protect you from the latest trend in electronic terrorism: WinNuke, Floods, and Stack Attacks. These forms of attack usually come up when you are chatting via mIRC or ICQ so you'd better think it over before using these applications (mIRC and ICQ are software programs, NOT web sites). However, these attacks may also occur over the Web. A PC firewall is like having an elite staff of bodyguards with you 24/7.

You'd never believe how comforting it is to see that "FIRE-WALL ACTIVATED" message come up after you run these programs. It's a good feeling.

THE BIG PHAKE-OUT

Picture yourself in a busy airport; the hustle and bustle is amazing. You need to make a call. You spot a bank of telephones under a bank of flight information monitors. Ah, good, one's open. You make your way through the crowd and . . . yes! . . . the phone is still free. You get close enough to smell the people on the other phone and are soon close enough to detect that the one closest to you hasn't taken a bath in a week. Great. Just get that call outta the way and . . .

But the phone's ringing. A puzzled frown comes over your face; should you let it ring? Pick it up? And say what? "Phil's not here right now, Ryhad, can I give him your number?" Good, it finally stops while you're muddling over your options. And a good thing, too, the BO is really making a comeback. You pick up the phone and let its soothing dial tone sing you a little song while you rummage your calling card out of your wallet.

You pause. You heard about this on TV. Is someone standing over your shoulder? You'd better make sure. You do the increasingly common, I'm-hip-to-the-street side-to-side glance. Clear. Good. Now you punch in that PIN with total impunity. Congratulations–you're super-safe!

Time passes. A week or two later you're at home, idling through the mail when THE BILL comes: the telephone bill, that is. You open it with trace memory of that airport call being several dollars more than what you would like to pay each month . . . but it's not a real prob–

You stop cold. The bill is several thousand dollars long. Wayyyyy long. Calls to Saudi Arabia. Afghanistan. Cities that look like strings of random consonants. Hours of calls. Hours. The airport. Someone nailed you.

How? Like this: the dial-tone was a fake. The mother-of-all fakes. It was generated with a DTMF (dial-tone modulation frequency generator). The source? A run-down apartment in St. Louis, or Chicago, or LA. Who knows? A DTMF? Just another little black box that can be ordered over the Web or from a traditional mail order "electronic security firm." It generates a dial-tone . . . and has a *tape recorder* built right in. What does it record? YOU. Everything you punch in: it's all being taped in that apartment. Oh, don't worry, they could care less about who you call; they stop the tape right after you dial and are waiting for your connection. And these lads are slick; they'll send you a bogus "the number you are calling has been disconnected" recording so you can hang up and try again. The results? Your card is stolen but your call goes through on the second try. You're none the wiser.

That ringing? That was the bad guys forcing a connection to take place with their funky little box. When you hear that dial-tone, that's just the box, you see. Your ass was theirs from the moment you saw that distant phone.

Can this happen anyplace else? YES, which is why I mention the whole process here. It can be done to steal your *password* for a computer system instead of the hackneyed calling card pin number. How? Yes, I thought you'd like to know. They use a fake, but instead of a dial-tone they fake a computer screen. Can't happen? Oh, yes it can, sweety, yes it can. A "computer screen" is just a GUI (graphical user interface) and can easily be duplicated using a simple language such as Visual Basic. VB is a programming language so intuitive and fun to use that *anyone* (and I do mean anyone) can "build" computer screens to look and act like the real thing. Is it difficult to program in all those pretty and complex "Navigator" graphics and buttons? Of course not; they can be copied from the actual screen itself with a *screenshot* (which usually amounts to using "Print Screen" on your keyboard). These "shots" are then doctored as necessary with MicroSoft's "Paint." Yes, this game is so simple it isn't necessary in the slightest to use a fancy-ass high end piece of software like "PhotoShop" to get the wet-work done.

For instance, if you run your Web browser at home, you'll notice the familiar "Dial-Up Connection" box come up, which prompts you for the password and username. Do you trust it? Well from home, of course. But on the road? In a large, anonymous university computer center? At your job? With your computer in the open? It would be child's play, it really would be, for anyone with just a modicum of know-how using Visual Basic to "write" a fake *Dial-Up screen* and have it come up right on the proverbial dime. This is all done under Windows and with no modifications of the operating system (Windows) or any safeguards being overridden. An easy way to make sure this gets the goods would be to delete or hide the *real* browser software in place of the *fakeware*, forcing the user to be sucked into the scam. Then you would just be running the fake all the way though. An equivalent to the "wrong number" recording? After entering in your password an unexpected "reboot" may take place, deleting the fake and restarting the computer. This would hide the criminal's tracks quite nicely.

The password may *still* come up in straight asterisks (********), but this is just the bad boys being cute. It's not encrypted like the real thing in any manner. What you type in will come to them, usually stored on the computer's hard-drive for later extraction in mass quantities, as clear as the daylight coming through a window pane . . . pardon the atrocious pun.

This is a very real and very effective threat to security. It may well be just a high-tech version of shoving a piece of cardboard in the coin-return slot of a candy machine, but it works all the same. In fact, at the school I went to, faked *Telnet sessions* were so common the university advised everyone not to Telnet in a general (public) lab. To be safe you had to do it from your home dial-up, where the software couldn't be tampered with.

Shew! So now you can't even pick up a ringing phone without paranoia consuming your entire life. Welcome to the 21st century! Now go home.

THE LAST THING

The best home-made protection system available for your connected PC (via modem to the Internet) is most certainly of the Frankenstein variety. Simply put, you cobble together all the crackz, appz, and proxies you can beg, borrow, or steal and run them *right on top of one another.* Here's an example.

My friend has the best state-of-the-art Invisibility Kit going on his computer as of this writing. Before *even considering* going on-line, he fires up ConSeal PC FireWall (cracked) to beat any intrusion attempts by evil Java (see *The Ultimate Internet Terrorist*), unauthorized cookies, and/or Nuke attempts. He has Norton CrashGuard (flat-out stolen off the Web) to prevent system crashes in case he is in a sweet-as-sugar FTP site and the deal goes sour on him. He *always* turns on the proxy server under Netscape before he surfs. Like the cherry on top, my friend has Norton Anti-Virus 6.0 (cracked) permanently installed in resident RAM to foil any infestations of e-cockroaches, regardless of whether he's surfing or not.

How does my friend know all of this good stuff is working? Well, when a virus *does* come over the Web (and they do, they do) all of his security appz go off like the Fourth of July. They blossom over one another in cascading windows filled with the same ALERT ALERT ALERT message flowering all over the screen. That's a good feeling. If one doesn't catch it, the others will. That's the power of tiered security. It's a good thing; take it from someone who knows.

So you see, my friend, as cheap as he is, is quite well protected by this *four-tier protection system*. (Again, this consists of a decent firewall, anticrasher utility, antivirus program, and using proxy server). He surfs with confidence . . . but he never forgets that if someone really wants his little ass, he just may wind up in deep shit. He never e-mail bombs from his home PC regardless of what safeguards he has in place and wouldn't even *think* about threatening someone from that same PC. My friend knows that someone clever may break any security system, no matter how elaborate, with enough technology behind him or her. Most importantly, my friend wants you to follow his example . . .

ELECTRONIC LIFE RAFTS–FOUR WAYS TO SAVE YOUR OWN ASS

Below I list four programs I feel no one in this day and age of techno-paranoia should be without. Everyone told me I should use three or five . . . not four, but screw them! Four it is!

Use these at your own discretion and risk. I cannot make decisions for you. I can only give you information and hope to hell that you have the common sense to know when to hold 'em and know when to fold 'em, as the great philosopher Kenny Rogers once sang.

Norton CrashGuard (any version)–This program will flat-out save your life someday. It will intercept just about any crash you can think of and give you the option of terminating the offending application, repairing it (don't hold your breath), or at least giving you 15 seconds or so in which you can save any information to disk.

@Guard (version 2.0 or higher)–Do you sleep safely at night knowing anyone can break into your PC while on the WWW? Do you? I don't. I use @Guard to make sure I don't have my head up my ass some night when a hacker decides I'M THE ONE he's got to smoke right there and then. @Guard functions as a firewall (as discussed elsewhere), a virus shield, and a cookie blocker. And it actually works! That's the part that always gets me: it performs as advertised.

Norton Anti-Virus (version 4.0 or higher)–I don't like the idea of waking up some day, going to the computer, and finding my hard drive formatted because it's Michelangelo's birthday. Norton AV will prevent this. McAfee V Shield will also do the trick . . . maybe. Norton gets it every time.

Secure-It / PC Security / softSentry (any 32-bit versions)–Any one of these . . . special . . . applications will encrypt (and hide) your files from prying eyes. (Imagine your wife's wide-eyed horror when she finds those cum facial JPEGs someday.) Certain ones will prevent browsing/modifying directories at your discretion. All have some form of *shred* capability as well. Shred first encrypts, then randomly scrambles, *then* deletes the files you determine to be too hot to keep around for long. I hope Oliver North is reading this . . .

CHAPTER FIVE

THE SUPER VIRUS

A Tour of Hell for Computers . . . and Their Owners

RUMORS. THE INTERNET (specifically the WWW) and all that dwell within feast on them. Hell, the Internet *gorges* itself sick on rumors. Entire Web rings (not just individual sites) are devoted to rumors and rumor generation. Everything from how Chelsea Clinton masterminds the "One World Government" to George Bush being the actual Anti-Christ (the actual embodiment, mind you) is here. The "Drudge Report" is perhaps the most widely known of these Web sites and, shockingly, being given serious air by the networks. Entertainment sells. Truth is, apparently, for idiots. Other sites on the WWW specialize in "Area 51"-style gossip circles where the possibility is *never* discounted that the bodies of "space aliens" reside within a secret base in Nevada. Well, if you're 9 years old I guess you can believe that. Me, I think they build spy satellites and expose the workers to chemicals used to make the solar panels. But I don't want to ruin this section by such bogus rumors.

I want to show you the real thing.

And yes! How ironic it is indeed that the longest-lived rumor on the Internet turns out to be true . . . a rumor so hackneyed and publicized in the mainstream media that no one takes it seriously. Well, *almost* no one . . .

Its existence has been given many, many incarnations over the decades. Some think of it as the "Loch Ness Monster" of the computer world, a rarely glimpsed specter of sheer madness. Others dismiss it as a demented hacker's ravings, they way we do if someone insists he saw a pack of velcioraptors roaming around Manhattan Island the day before yesterday. Some simply hear it, process it through their own experiences, and come down neither on one side or another; sort of the high-tech form of "I'll believe it when—and if—I see it, not a moment before." Computer researchers and other academics know it's there . . . although few in their ranks (if any) have actually witnessed this aberration from Hell first-hand. It's like the giant-squid from their point of view: we know it's there, it's just a matter of time until someone catches one . . .

Well, we caught one. And here it is. Yes, I'm actually going to let you glimpse it for a moment–a moment that will haunt you to your grave. Others will vigorously disagree with the wisdom of this action but why shouldn't I, really? You paid your admission fee, fair and square, and like PT Barnum I will gladly give you all that you paid for. And also like that master showman, you may get more than you bargained for. I'll pry up the lid of this Ultimate Pandora's Box and let you peek in for a second–nothing more. There's a long line in front of the freak show today, and everyone's got to get a glimpse.

You see, this creature will torture you both day and night, never leaving your thoughts for long. Some among you will be struck mad by this spectacle and wish to harness it yourself; a perverted version of the Greek goddess so lovely she must be won at any cost. Most will fail. But some will capture it for themselves, only to release it on mankind, destroying everything in its path. Much like the magical ring from the classic J.R.R. Tolkien story of decades ago, the Super Virus will consume its possessor, bending him to its own malevolent ends.

You see, nothing can stop the Super Virus. Nothing.

- It cannot be detected by any means.
- It knows not a shred of mercy or compassion.
- It cannot be removed from its "host" by any method known to science.
- Once free, it will destroy with total impunity.
- The Super Virus, once started, cannot be stopped or interrupted.
- Cutting the power to a computer system will have no effect.

Sound like fun? Well, step into my office, lad, there's something in here I want to show you.

BEGINNINGS

We can't jump right into this–it's just too complex. I can't give you the secret just yet. Your mortal mind would shatter the instant it is revealed. Ever wonder what it would feel like to be sucked into a black hole? Your body would be torn apart at the speed of light, every fiber of your being stretched into an endless black abyss. But we can sneak up on it. We can observe the black hole from a distance. At least, that's what I tell myself. Sometimes it works. But sometimes you get sucked in anyway.

A virus damages your computer by replicating itself. Replication itself is often more than enough to cause irreparable damage. A hard drive can be choked to death by random bits of data swarming over every sector and track.

But people got smart to this in the roaring '90s. They developed software to detect and, God save us all, actually clean virii from a system. Sometimes it worked. More often than not it was high-tech shark repellent, giving peace of mind rather than hard results. Then McAfee and Norton came on the scene and gave real results. People became complacent. They liked what they saw. They were safe at last.

A NEW DAY

But they aren't safe for long. As I pointed out in *The Ultimate Internet Terrorist*, the field of technology and, more specifically, technology-based crime, is an ever-changing battlefield. No sooner may one side claim victory than its counter will assault it from the rear, driving it to earth. Hence the next move in the grand game of cyber-chess. A new dawn has come for those cyber-terrorists for which only the best in high-tech weapons will do.

Gentlemen, I present to you the Super Virus. It is merely a line of code that deletes disk data. Alternatively, it may imprint debug strings on the disk or format the disk completely. Such a line of code is not technically speaking a virus at all, since it does

```
Private Button_Click()

        Disk = "c:\*.*"

        Rem Kill Disk

        End_Message

End_Sub


Private Sub End_Message()

        Label = "All Done!"

End_Sub
```

Figure 15. Note the unbelievably simple programming code necessary to create the 21st century Super Virus under Visual Basic. A rudimentary knowledge of VB is helpful but not vital. The on-line tutorial provided with the MS Visual Basic package is adequate for this job. Note the remarks in green and self-contained modules. The word "Kill" is an actual command in VB. Makes you wonder whose side MS is on, doesn't it?

not reproduce itself . . . and is not detectable by any means. Code? Yes, the Super Virus may be written in any brand application source from C++ to Visual Basic. Hell, you could even write my Super Virus in Assembler if you cared to.

The Super Virus we'll tour here is of the Visual Basic (VB) variety. This is done for several reasons. First, VB is easy; you can pick it up in a day or so with the tutorial. Second (and most importantly), the compiler and editor are in the same application. This simply means you can write the program (the Super Virus) and compile it into an .exe form with the same program. Third, the application (Microsoft Visual Basic) is dirt cheap, and nearly everyone can get their conniving little hands on it. Is that true with C++? Not really. *You* may think it is, but to a lot of people C and its cognates are not merely foreign languages but things from Dimension X. (Pro coders out there know where I'm coming from.)

After compiling such a simple program, a hacker could

then upload it to any and all freeware or shareware sites on the WWW. He would of course name his creation something useful and brief . . . something *you* might find attractive and easy to use. The name I've chosen here ("Registry Editor 98") contains all those elements. It is a prime candidate for such a Trojan Horse. Once you download and scan (McAfee or Norton, they will both fail, so it makes not a shred of difference) the Trojan Horse/Super Virus, you will immediately want to run it by clicking on it. Scanning the program for viruses will be the next-to-last thing your computer will ever do. Clicking on "start" *will* be the last thing your computer ever sees (examine the source code).

Alternate designs on this basic theme would be the modification of the source to *automatically* "Kill" your hard drive upon execution (hence no "start" button would be necessary). Believe it or not, some hackers often find it cute to drop clues in the GUI ("Form" if you use Visual Basic). Such clues sometimes take the form of the words "Sucker!" in the top-left hand portion of the GUI (replacing "Registry Editor 98"). You should *always* respect such a clue! Immediately exit the program by hitting ctrl-alt-del on your keyboard and then *ending* the task (the Trojan Horse). Do not attempt to use File – Exit from the Super Virus! The hacker, for obvious reasons, almost always traps that route.

Note that the code I have provided may need some retooling if you want to get around Windows 95/98 Recycle bin and executable fail-safe dialogue boxes. (I would suggest using "format" instead of deleting the files individually, for instance. There are other ways that you may experiment with.)

I NEVER TOLD YOU ANY OF THIS

That's right. You may have heard voices in your head or sounds sighing through the eaves . . . but you certainly didn't hear it from this white boy. No siree, Bob.

Kurt Saxon once told me that information is power. Whether it's from this book or my last one, it's power, and you can destroy with it if you so desire. I cannot stop you. You may prepare yourself for the dangers that lurk in this electronic nightmare world, and I hope you stay safe, but I cannot guarantee that you will.

I never told you any of this.

If a man reads a book and blows up the U.S. embassy in Kenya or reads *Catcher in the Rye* and then shoots John Lennon in the face, hey, it's his ticket to the chair, not mine. You will prosper if you use your newfound power to create . . . and karma will destroy you as you destroy in turn if you decide to follow that path.

I never told you any of this. It's not my call; it's yours.

Choose wisely, for this is a one-way street: I can only teach. And you can only listen.

Peace out homies,

Robert Merkle

APPENDIX
Bloody Affairs Department

AHHHH YES, ALL RIGHT, I'LL CONFESS the best thing about Minnery's books weren't the main text at all. No, no, the best part was the quaint little appendix at the end of each one: "Bloody Affairs Department." Such was his colorful code phrase for a treasure chest stuffed with odds and ends, trinkets that didn't quite fit in the main text, forbidden secrets best left unsaid. Here you could've learned how to make an invisible dagger from glass that was razor-sharp and able to penetrate any body armor known (the military still considers this a secret, by the way), do some funky kitchen-chemistry like mixing explosive cocktails from a pack of cigarettes and tree stump remover, even learn to kill a sentry with one cupped blow to the ear. These were awesome things . . . secret things.

I've given the Bloody Affairs Department a high-tech twist here, and, while the sentry may not be defeated with a one-strike kill, you'll learn a trick or two to stay ahead of the uninitiated on the Information Superhighway . . . Enjoy!

★ ★ ★ ★

A sneaky way to safely communicate with those of your . . . associates . . . in the underground is to pervert Web mail services. Here's the twist: create just ONE e-mail account, and let your buddies know the password. Send e-mail to yourself with an appropriate subject field so they know whom it's for.

You should use this trick in conjunction with a server outside the United States, and preferably in a foreign language. Such sites may be found in Mexico and Spain quite readily. Remember, even though you will need to hunt and peck for the appropriate commands (assuming you don't know any Spanish), no one will object to your sending yourself e-mail in English.

The beauty is that the message travel is sharply curtailed; server-to-server communication is almost nonexistent, thus increasing the odds of being undetected.

★ ★ ★ ★

Need to scare the holy fuck out of someone? A cute trick is to set up a BLUE SCREEN OF DEATH (system screen) screen saver on someone's computer without his or her knowledge. Set the timer for 1 minute. This screen saver only shuts off with a keystroke (it ignores mouse clicks, thus adding to the confusion). And it won't deactivate with a reboot—no matter how many times the mark attempts to resolve his "problem." For the program, go to http://www.sysinternals.com/bluescrn.htm.

★ ★ ★ ★

Try a commercial program called "Absolute Security Standard" to encrypt e-mail attachments and other material you send out over the 'net (including private stuff you post for download on your WWW site if you have one). The good thing is the person on the other end DOES NOT need the program; he only needs a password to decrypt your stuff. Another title to try is "Norton's Secret Stuff."

★ ★ ★ ★

I came back to the computer from a quick trip to the 7-11 to discover yet another change in information super-freedom:

you may now download just-released-to-the-theater feature length movies on the 'net. These are type .vivo/.viv files (in a similar manner as the .mp3 formatted files) and require a special player. The player (called a VIVO Player) is readily available on the Web and costs nothing.

The bad news? Download times: a typical movie is 200 megs long and sometimes 300. This equates (assuming a 28.8 connection) to around 20 hours of download time. FTP sites are the only place to hunt for these treasure chests. Warez sites on the Web (such as WarezNation.com and KickassWarez.com) will usually have pointers to such sites.

A typical menu will have Gamez, Appz, MP3z and Videoz. A typical VIVO file will look like this: privateryan.viv 398,123,456 bytes.

That's nearly four hundred megs! Good f*!&%king luck!

★ ★ ★ ★

Concerning hard-drive space, you need to be aware that you don't always get what you pay for. Case in point: my first slave drive was-out-of-the-box rated at 6.5 gig. Great, I thought, no trouble using that extra one-half gig; no trouble at all. After I formatted the disk and partitioned it I was left with 6.0 gig. Man, I just about hit the ceiling. An entire half gig gone up in smoke.

Next stop? Calling the good people at Seagate, whom I bought the drive from. After several minutes of generally good-natured chatter about over-head bytes and head-platter assemblies I stuck them with the question: where the hell did my 500 megs go?

Their answer: the partition stole it. And it's a completely normal situation. They went on to tell me that ALL drives do this. Learning from my experience, as a general rule of thumb you need to disregard the decimal portion of hard-disk space. A 8.7 GB is just 8 gigs. A 3.2 is 3.0. A 10.9 combs out to 10 on the nose.

Incidentally this also holds for CD-R (Compact Disc

Recordable) people. Those neat shiny disks are rated at 650 MB so you're gonna get every penny...right? Not exactly. You got it worse. After you format and partition you'll be left with 480 MB usable.

Start screaming.

★ ★ ★ ★

Are you a two-dimensional hacker? Consider: say you want into someone's desktop . . . really, really bad. And, of course, being no dummies, they have it locked with something fairly professional like FoolProof. Or—far worse—a pull-out card lock that won't even let you start the thing without the proper micro-tag signature (it looks exactly like a credit card and you can actually buy such a thing for around $100). You could try all the tricks in *the Ultimate Internet Terroristt*, but you still couldn't get through (remember the "slammer disk"?).

Do you give up? You will if you only think along limited lines.

But the next-step-up hacker is the electronic equivalent of a second-story cat burglar. He's got brains and some specialized skills. Think how you would solve such a dilemma before reading my solution.

Stumped? Answer: you go physical. Simply unplug the thing, unscrew the hood, and rip out the hard drive by the ears. Then attach it to another system as a slave drive (a secondary hard disk) to copy/read the goodies. This method will get around boot-up protection schemes of all manner, race, religion, color, and creed.

Begin to think along these "third-dimensional" lines yourself and see how it solves lots of life's little . . . problems.

ABOUT THE AUTHOR

ROBERT MERKLE IS A LIFE-LONG HACKER. His best-selling first book, *The Ultimate Internet Terrorist,* was the culmination of nearly 15 years of hacking nastiness. *The Ultimate Internet Bandit* is his second book.

Merkle began exploring the nasty underbelly of the computer scene around 1984 ("Back when the World Wide Web was a telephone handset and a Commodore 64," he reminisces.") Now he enjoys the luxuries of the 21st century, keeping his ear closely in tune to the Internet underground.

To those who doubt there exists a high-tech Mafia, he says, "Get on the 'net and explore for yourself. I can't help but quote from the movie *Blade*: 'There is another world beneath this sugar-coated topping—the real world.'"

Merkle is currently working for a Fortune 500 company while finishing up his degree at a major university in the Midwest. He desperately tells anyone who will listen (including his employer) that he'll graduate "any day now"—which he's been saying for the last seven years.

In between writing for Paladin and generally causing trouble on the

Information Superhighway, Merkle acts as a security consultant on a word-of-mouth basis and always in the deeply shadowed alleys and backstreets of the 'net.

When asked if he will ever stop raiding the Internet for more cracked software, Merkle simply laughs, "Yep. When Janet Reno's Storm Troopers blast into my dorm room and pry my cold, dead fingers off the keyboard."

We hope that doesn't happen.